THE GOLDEN AGE OF

The Blues

Instrumentals
with Vocal
Accompaniment

Long Playing

TWENTY CLASSIC BLUES TRACKS

p 2009
Compendium Publishing Ltd.

THE GOLDEN AGE OF
The Blues

THE GOLDEN AGE OF
The Blues

RICHARD HAVERS & RICHARD EVANS

CHARTWELL
BOOKS, INC.

Published in 2009 by Compendium Publishing,
43 Frith Street, London W1D 4SA, United Kingdom.

CHARTWELL BOOKS, INC.
A Division of
BOOK SALES, INC.
276 Fifth Avenue Suite 206
New York, New York 10001

Copyright © 2009 by Compendium Publishing Ltd.,
43 Frith Street, London W1D 4SA

ISBN 13: 978-0-7858-2499-2
ISBN 10: 0-7858-2499-5

The information in this book is true and complete to the best
of our knowledge. All recommendations are made without
any guarantee on the part of the Authors or Publisher, who
also disclaim any liability incurred in connection with the use
of this data or specific details.

We recognize, further, that some words, model names, and
designations mentioned herein are the property of the
trademark holder. We use them for identification purposes
only. This is not an official publication.

Compiled, written and designed by
Richard Havers and Richard Evans.

All Internet site information provided was correct when
provided by the Authors. The Publisher can accept no
responsibility for this information becoming incorrect.

Printed and bound in China

PHOTOGRAPHY

Every effort has been made to trace the copyright holders. Compendium Publishing
apologizes for any unintentional omissions, and would be pleased, if any such case
should arise, to add an appropriate acknowledgement in future editions.

4: 42-18455063 © Corbis; 6: BE079068 © Bettmann/Corbis; 8: IH106671 © Corbis;
20: AY008809 © Raymond Gehman/Corbis; 45: QX001019 © Terry Cryer/Corbis;
46: U1296806INP © Bettmann/Corbis; 52: H185966 © Corbis; 55: BE004336
© Bettmann/Corbis; 114: 42-19071386 © Joel Brodsky/Corbis; 118: 42-17367791
© Michael Ochs Archives/Corbis; 137: 42-16507492 © Michael Ochs Archives/Corbis;
148: QX001090 © Terry Cryer/Corbis; 152: 75865 © Randy Faris/Corbis; 154: PN012462
© Neal Preston/Corbis; 157: 2-16507491 © Michael Ochs Archives/Corbis;
160: UT0081045 © Reuters/Corbis; 172: 42-17853556 © Michael Ochs Archives/Corbis;
180: 42-16887134 © Michael Ochs Archives/Corbis; 184: 42-17728262 © Deborah
Feingold/Corbis; 187: 42-18128958 © Gavin Hellier/JAI/Corbis;
22: © The Grainger Collection / TopFoto
25, 66, 69, 75, 77, 79, 107, 110: © Michael Ochs Archives/Getty Images
92: © GAB Archives/Redferns; 95: © Jan Persson/Redferns; 101: © Gilles Petard
Collection/Redferns; 124, 129: © Deltahaze Corporation/Redferns; 140: © David
Redfern/Redferns; 147: © BBC Photo Library/Redferns; 167: © GEMS/Redferns;
176: © Echoes Archives/Redferns
30, 38, 60, 84, 144, 165: © The Dix Archive
14, 35, 50, 82: © Richard Havers
24, 28, 32, 36, 42, 58, 64, 72, 89, 90, 96, 98, 104, 112, 121, 122, 132, 134, 142, 162, 170, 178,
191: © Richard Evans

Contents

The Birth of the Blues

"When you lay down at night, turning from one side of the bed to the other and can't sleep, what's the matter? Blues got you."
~ *Lead Belly*

IT WAS 1619, the year before the Pilgrim Fathers landed at Plymouth, Massachusetts that the first slaves arrived in North America from Africa. Their long, often terrifying, journey by ship saw many men, women and children die before reaching their new 'homes.' Those that survived this awful ordeal were present at the birth of what we call the blues.

Today television programs tell us about "the amazing sounds to be heard in Africa." They are referring to the sounds of nature; of animals, birds, insects, even the sounds of the heat. This is what has inspired the African musician for many millennia. African music is no different to any other music – there are work songs, lullabies, religious and military and songs just for enjoying.

African music is dominated by the call-and-response form, which strongly influenced blues and jazz. The slaves took nothing with them, no musical instruments and no written music. However, African music is not written down, it is purely an oral tradition, allowing it to travel freely in the minds of the slaves; which meant that hundreds of years later the blues were able to develop through a musical tradition passed down the generations.

African music did not always meet with the approval of the European colonists; early references talk about the unpleasant nature of African singing. Unsurprisingly, it was not long before the traditional music of Africa and the ballads, airs, hymns, and psalms, as well as the instruments on which to play them taken to the Colonies by the European settlers, began influencing one another. By the early 19th century, from its rural roots, the African-influenced music began to spread to the cities in both the north and south, nowhere more so than in New Orleans. There were European-style bands, as well as slave orchestras and brass bands. Out of these divergent musical traditions, the black orchestras, brass bands, Creole singing and dance musicians all allied to the free-spirited dance and rhythms of the Place Congo, was to come jazz. By 1834, the rich musical culture of New Orleans began to spread to the Mississippi Delta.

The Delta begins at Vicksburg, 300 miles from the mouth of the river, extending for 250 miles northward to Memphis. The vast almond-shaped alluvial plain was formed from thousands of years of flooding by the mighty Mississippi River in the west and the smaller Yazoo River in the east. Until 1820, the Delta was an undeveloped area of hardwood forest. Around 1835, settlers begun to clear it so that cotton could be grown. After the Civil War, plantations were developed throughout the Delta, creating an unrelenting environment that was the catalyst for the blues.

Today, many think that the South was a place made up entirely of white owners and their slaves, whereas only around 25% of Southern whites actually owned slaves. Another popular misconception is that there were only vast estates employing hundreds of slaves. In 1800 around 15% of owners had more than 20 slaves, while the majority of slaves lived on plantations that had from two or three to around 15 slaves. Neither was the plantation economy exclusively based on cotton; rice, sugar-cane and tobacco were also grown. When Mississippi entered the Union in 1817 there were 70,000 people living there, of whom 30,000 were black. By 1860 there were 791,000 people; 435,000 were black and most of them were slaves.

The end of the Civil War did not mean the end of the plantation economy. The plantations still existed, and blacks still provided the labor, but it was now through a system of tenant farming. Former slaves were allowed to farm the fields of the white landowners in return for a share of the crop when it was harvested. The landowners owned the tools, provided their clothing and also ran the stores where the workers bought their supplies. This iniquitous debt-creating system was called sharecropping. The influx of black workers continued right up until World War I, when blacks outnumbered whites by four to one. The feudal sharecropping system operated well into the 20th century, until the automated cotton harvester effectively ended the plantation economy in the 1950s.

Musically it was European folk songs and hymns that were a major influence on the black people. They produced a unique amalgam of African musical idioms with these European influences. First came the spirituals, a direct result of black men copying white gospel hymns. One significant difference between black spirituals and gospel hymns are the words, probably as a result of the somewhat limited vocabulary of the slaves. They used lyrical concepts borrowed from gospel hymns and simply adapted them to their own ends.

Many freed slaves sought work on the railroads, on steamboats, on mining, and lumber camps, and with the levee gangs; many of these men later found themselves in prison. They were incarcerated on the slightest pretext by southern whites that still thought of the former slaves as theirs to do with as they pleased. Both the railroad and the prison helped shape the black musical future. The first transcontinental railroad was completed in 1869 and throughout this post-war period many former slaves followed the railroad in search of work. From the railroads came a whole tradition of both black and white railroad songs. One of the most famous was 'John Henry'; the story of a 220-pound black rail hand who became a folk hero. It's a secular folk song with vestiges of the religious in the lyrics.

Music was subject to all these influences and during the second half of the 19th century it was changing and developing at a rapid rate. No doubt, it was in part due to the freeing of the slaves, but it must also have been because America changed too. The development of cities and the expansion of the nation, particularly through railroads, helped mould the musical map of America.

We'll never know who wrote the first blues song,

"African music is the key that unlocks the secrets of jazz." ~ *Rudi Blesh, jazz historian*

" ...the future music of this country must be founded on... the Negro melodies."

~ composer Antonin Dvorak in 1893

even 'wrote' is a misnomer as no one actually wrote it, the blues developed through the complex oral tradition of African-based music. Music developed rapidly during the last 40 years of the 19th century, a development made more difficult as there was no TV, radio, CDs, records, tapes or any other process for hearing recorded music; it literally spread through word of mouth. Songs were changed, altered and 'improved' upon as they made their journey throughout America.

Naturally, this process was nowhere more piecemeal than in the countryside. Devoid of theatres or other places to hear music, it was the itinerant musician and collective singing in family or other groups that helped pass along all manner of songs.

Black men working in fields, in prison gangs, on railroads or in any lowly job made their own entertainment. For them, a radio sitting on the workbench or placed next to them in a field was totally unimaginable. Hollering was just one form of singing; we have only word of mouth to tell us what these people sang about to relieve the monotony of their daily grind.

Many of the most obvious features of jazz are derived directly from the blues, but whereas the blues are primarily a vocal style, jazz replaces the voice with instruments. Personality is what makes great jazz and blues; it is a performance of an individualistic nature that is transcendent. Jazz, like the blues, requires free expression and charismatic playing to lift performers and performances above and beyond the confines of the style.

It was in 1903 that W.C. Handy, the self-styled 'Father of the Blues', was working in Clarksdale as the Director of the Knights of Pythias Band that he first heard 'the blues.' However, there's conjecture that by 1870 the blues were already well established; even regional forms persisted, it would have been surprising if they had not, given the way that music had to 'travel.' It is arguable that the blues were also turning up in many of the Southern cities well before this time, 'Buddy Bolden's Blues,' for example dates from the mid-1890s. Ten years or so later, a musician by the name of Harrison Barnes went to New Orleans to play the piano in a brothel, just off Canal Street. " They were slow tunes, unhappy. They was what they call the blues now, only they called them ditties in them days."

This may explain some of the possible confusion. What a particular musical style was called was not something that people in the rural South were much bothered by. They were just tunes or songs to be sung, music made to entertain, and sometimes even to assist them while going about their everyday lives. Poor Southern blacks and whites were just getting on with life, not in the least bit imagining that future generations would be looking into their culture, trying to analyze the subtle nuances of musical form.

A few years before Handy met the blues at Tutwiler, near Clarksdale, a white archaeologist, Charles Peabody, along with a team of black diggers, was excavating at a site near Stovall, Mississippi. He recorded in his writings that his black workers sang improvized songs that were blues in form. Between 1905 and 1908 Howard Odum, a folklorist who later published a large collection of black folksongs, traveled throughout the Delta and Georgia on a field trip. More than half of the songs he noted were blues and much of the lyrical content in his collection appeared in blues songs that were recorded much later on. What is particularly interesting about Odum is the fact that he tells us how and where these songs were sung; in particular after church, at social gatherings, dances, on the front stoops of shotgun shacks or around the fireside. The blues had likely been around for a long time before Odum started his research.

Using the word 'blue' to describe a feeling or a mood goes back to the 16th century; by the 19th century it was variously used to describe a fit of depression, boredom or sheer unhappiness, and it was particularly associated with the black population. By 1912, when Handy published 'The Memphis Blues,' which ironically is not a blues tune but an instrumental cakewalk, the fad for using the word 'blues' was already several years old.

In structure and content the blues form is fairly standard, although it's often less than rigidly adhered to. The blues stanza tends to be in eight or twelve bars, although there can be in many other permutations... even twelve-and-a-half! What is important to the singer is the fact that the song should sound 'right.' Along with the form of the stanza go the flattened third and seventh notes, which give the blues its sound; these have become known as 'blue notes.'

Idiosyncratic singing styles are another typical aspect of the blues. Often the last word or syllable is dropped from the end of a line, creating a loose and unfinished sound to the performance. A partial explanation of this could lie in the fact that many of the songs have their origins in the call-and-response mechanism of the work song or spiritual. The 'chorus' would often finish a line that had been started by the 'caller'.

The blues are not exclusively about complaints and worries; they're just as likely to be about sex or social comment. In actual fact the blues are often filled with a lot of humor. But given the situation that most black people found themselves after the Civil War and the early years of the 20th century it is hardly surprising that there is an ample dose of the downbeat.

When you play the CD, if you are struck by nothing else you will be touched by the singers' commitment to their craft, the depth of their emotion and the sheer potency of feeling... that is what the blues is all about.

"Blues is a natural fact, something that a fellow lives. If you don't live it, you don't have it." ~ *Big Bill Broonzy*

A Blues Timeline

1517 The Spanish take the first slaves to America.

1619 The first boatload of slaves arrives in Virginia.

1700 28,000 African slaves are in the North American Colonies.

1760 325,800 African slaves are in the American Colonies.

1769 First reference to Negro songs in the theatre: 'Dear Heart what a terrible Life I am Led' is performed in New York.

1774 Thomas Jefferson makes reference to the abolition of slavery as a goal of the colonialists. An Englishman travelling in Maryland makes reference to a banjo being used at a Negro ball.

1791 A black-face minstrel show is performed in New Orleans by a company of slaves; their black faces are blacked up!

1800 One million blacks in the U.S.A. – 18.9% of the total population.

VALUABLE GANG OF YOUNG
NEGROES
By JOS. A. BEARD.
Will be sold at Auction,
ON WEDNESDAY, 25TH INST.
At 12 o'clock, at Banks' Arcade,
17 Valuable Young Negroes,
Men and Women, Field Hands,
Sold for no fault; with the best
city guarantees.
Sale Positive
and without reserve!
TERMS CASH.
New Orleans, March 24, 1840.

1808 One million African slaves are in the U.S.A.

1823 Mississippi passes laws that prevent teaching blacks to read and write.

1850 3.6 million blacks in the U.S.A. – 15.7% of the total population.

1861 The beginning of the Civil War.

1865 The end of the Civil War. Lincoln assassinated.

1885 Papa Charlie Jackson born.

1894 'Big' Gibson guitars start to be manufactured. Bessie Smith is born.

1903 Charles Peabody writes down lyrics to 'blues' songs his 'diggers' sing while they work at Stovall's Plantation.

1905 The Memphis Players, the first modern jazz band, make their debut.

1909 W.C. Handy writes the first blues song, a campaign theme for the notorious Memphis mayor

The Memphis Blues
or
(Mister Crump)
By W. C. HANDY

'Boss' Crump, called 'Boss Crump Blues.' It's published in 1912 as 'The Memphis Blues.'

1910 The word 'blues' to apply to music is in fairly common use. The National Association for the Advancement of Colored People (NAACP) is formed.

1912 WC Handy's 'The Memphis Blues' is published. Some 'bluesologists' claim (rather dubiously), that the first blues song ever written down was 'Dallas Blues,' published in 1912 by Hart Wand, a white violinist from Oklahoma City.

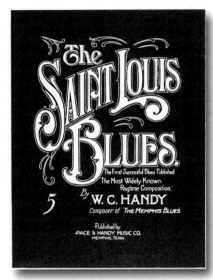

1913 Robert Wilkins, a country blues artist from Mississippi, begins his career while entertaining whites and blacks with a similar collection of songs.

1914 W.C.Handy publishes 'The Saint Louis Blues.'

1915 The publication of 'Jelly Roll Blues,' a jazz arrangement by Ferdinand 'Jelly Roll' Morton.

1917 The *Chicago Defender* urges blacks to 'flee the south.'

W.C. Handy publishes 'Beale Street Blues.'

1919 Race riots in Chicago.

1920 Prohibition begins. Mamie Smith records 'Crazy Blues' for Okeh Records. The first record to sell a million, 'Whispering,' played by the Mayfair Dance Orchestra and conducted by George Byng. AM Radio begins broadcasting with 'regularly scheduled programming.'

1921 Ethel Waters makes her first recording for Harry Pace's Black Swan jazz label.

1923 Bessie Smith's 'Down Hearted Blues' sells 800,000 copies.

1924 Papa Charlie Jackson records 'Papa's Lawdy Lawdy Blues.'

1925 Blind Lemon Jefferson became the first southern self-accompanied folk blues artist to succeed commercially on records.

1926 Blind Lemon Jefferson's 'That Black Snake Moan' is released. His popularity shows the record companies that a rural blues market exists.

1927 First recordings by the 'Father of Country Music,' Jimmie Rodgers.
When the AC plug-in set with single-knob tuning is launched, radio really takes off among the general population.
The birth of the 'automatic phonograph' or juke box, manufactured by AMI.

1928 *Billboard* magazine publishes its first music chart of performed songs.

1929 The Wall Street Crash, and the beginning of the Depression.
Blind Lemon Jefferson records 'Black Snake Moan #2.'

1932 25% of the U.S.A.'s labour force out of work..

1933 Prohibition ends.

1934 Lead Belly released from prison again, with help from John and Alan Lomax.

1935 Recovery from Depression.
Billboard magazine publishes its first chart of top-selling records.

1936 23 November: Robert Johnson makes his first recordings.

1937 30 June: Robert Johnson's last recordings.

1938 The first 'Spirituals to Swing' concert at New York's Carnegie Hall.

1940 FM Radio broadcasting begins.

1941 Alan Lomax records Muddy Waters at Stovall's Plantation in Rolling Fork, Mississippi.

1942 *Billboard* initiates the race chart, called the Harlem Hit Parade.
Radio station WJLD in Birmingham, Alabama goes totally black programming.

1944 Radio station WHAT in Philadelphia goes totally black programming.

1945 *Billboard* publishes the first album chart.

1947 Regular television programming begins on seven U.S. East Coast stations.

1948 WDIA in Memphis becomes the first station in the city to switch to all-black programming.
The long-playing record (LP) is introduced by Columbia Records.

1949 Lead Belly becomes the first blues artist to play in Europe when he appears in France.
31 March: RCA issues the first 45-rpm records.
The term 'rhythm & blues' is used rather than 'race records' for the first time.

1950 Leonard and Philip Chess found their label. Sam Phillips opens his

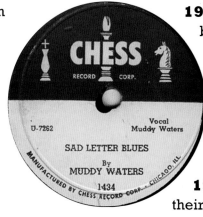

Memphis Recording Services.

1951 Elmore James records 'Dust My Broom'. Howlin' Wolf records 'Moanin' at Midnight' at Sun Studios in Memphis. Alan Freed's *Moon Dog House Rock'n'Roll Party* begins on WJW out of Cleveland, Ohio. June: The last No. 1 record on the *Billboard* R&B chart available only on 78-rpm is Jackie Brenston's 'Rocket 88' (Chess 1458).

1952 B.B. King's recording of Lowell Fulson's 'Three O'Clock Blues' tops the R&B chart.

1953 The first extended-play record (EP) is introduced.

1954 5 July: Elvis Presley, a truck driver from Tupelo, Mississippi, makes his first commercial recording in Sam Phillip's studio. In Britain, Lonnie Donegan records Leadbelly's 'Rock Island Line.'

1955 The 45-rpm single is the dominant format in the U.S.A.

1958 First stereo records

introduced.
1960 John Lee Hooker performs at the Newport Folk Festival.

1961 Columbia issues Robert Johnson's recordings on LP.

1962 The Beatles 'Love Me Do' is released. The first American Folk Blues Festivals tour Europe.

From this point on the blues became part of the mainstream as young white musicians and fans begin to embrace the music and seek out bluesmen from years ago that are still able to perform.

Overleaf: The statue of William Christopher 'W.C.' Handy, the 'Father of the Blues,' on Beale Street, Memphis, TN.

"The singer
repeated the
line three times,
accompanying
himself on the
guitar with the
weirdest music
I had ever heard."
~W.C. Handy

Lead Belly

"Perhaps this modern age is not liable to produce such a combination of genuine folk artist and virtuoso. Because nowadays when the artist becomes a virtuoso, there is normally a much greater tendency to cease being folk. But when Leadbelly rearranged a folk melody he had come across – he often did, for he had a wonderful ear for melody and rhythm – he did it in line with his own great folk traditions." ~ *Pete Seeger 1962*

NICKNAMES CAN SOMETIMES BE derogatory, sometimes totally apposite. In Huddie Ledbetter's case calling him Lead Belly or Leadbelly was just about perfect. If a man's nickname is indicative of his personality then no one could have been more aptly named. Ever since he found fame in the 1940s many have written his name as one word, but he liked it written as two, so who are we to argue with the man who claimed to know more songs than any other performer? He was also a convicted killer, a womanizer, and for white people in particular, in the post-World War II years Lead Belly was their conduit to the blues.

The man who provided the soundtrack to a journey through much of America's folk music tradition was christened Huddie William Ledbetter. He was born to sharecropping parents in 1888 in Mooringsport, Louisiana; his mother was part Cherokee Indian, and lived on a Louisiana plantation with his father Wess. When he was five the family moved to Texas. He left home when he was still very young and little is known of his early life, because Lead Belly was reluctant to talk about it. He met Blind Lemon Jefferson in 1915, and claims to have worked with him for a while, although his recollections were somewhat confused as to the precise date. In 1917, having already served time in prison for assault, Lead Belly shot and killed a man in Texas; at the time he was going by the name of Walter Boyd. He was sentenced to 33 years in jail and then, after he tried to escape, a further six years were added. In 1925 the resourceful Lead Belly earned a pardon from the Governor of Texas, Pat Neff, after he composed and sang a song

"Lead Belly was the most versatile of all singers in the Afro-American tradition and was deep-rooted in its folkways."
~ *Ross Russell,* Down Beat

pleading for his freedom… so the story goes. It seems more likely that he was released under a more normal program of freeing prisoners who were well behaved.

It was while Lead Belly was with Blind Lemon Jefferson that he had learned to play the 12-string guitar. Its rich tones as well as volume were ideal for playing in saloons; the Mexican musicians who were to be found all over Texas favored it. The 12-string perfectly complemented powerful and wonderfully rhythmic playing style in which he imitated the walking bass used by the barrelhouse piano players in Shreveport's red light district, down on Fannin Street.

In 1930 he was arrested once again, on an assault and attempted murder charge; this time he was sent to the Angola Prison Farm in Louisiana. In 1933 the folklorist, John Avery Lomax, who was travelling throughout the south with his son Alan, recording traditional songs and music for the Folk Song Archive of the Library of Congress, visited the prison and was captivated by Lead Belly's singing. The Lomaxes petitioned Louisiana governor O.K. Allen to pardon Lead Belly. Somewhat surprisingly, for a second time lightning did strike and he found himself free. He became the Lomax's chauffeur, as well as performing occasionally. He toured college towns with the folk-song hunters where he found he was greatly appreciated by the students. The Lomaxes introduced Lead Belly to the young, banjo-playing, Pete Seeger; this son of a famous musicologist became a firm friend.

Lead Belly decided to settle in New York in the mid-30s and issued his first commercial recordings in 1935 for the Arc label. Lead Belly got to know Josh White, the other darling of the left-wing New York crowd, and through Pete Seeger they both got to know Woody Guthrie. There is no question that Lead Belly was more popular with white audiences, and it was whites not blacks that bought the majority of his records. Lead Belly was even more influential than Josh White in allowing young white Americans and Europeans to access the blues, and the folk traditions of black America. Lead Belly was not a traditional blues singer, he was more of a songster; he performed blues, spirituals, dance tunes and folk ballads… anything his audiences

"I'm king of the 12-string guitar."
~ *Huddie 'Lead Belly' Ledbetter*

"He sang the blues wonderfully, but he was much bigger than that. He encompassed the whole black era, from square-dance calls to the blues of the 30s and 40s." ~ *Alan Lomax*

demanded he sing; fortunately, by his own admission, he knew around 500 songs. 'Gallis Pole,' 'Pick a Bale of Cotton,' 'John Hard,' 'Cottonfields,' and 'Mary Don't You Weep' all proved very popular. Not that his new friends seemed to calm his overheating temperament. In 1939 he served another jail term, for stabbing a man in a fight in Manhattan; this time in New York State Prison at Rikers Island, New York.

He also got to know Sonny Terry and Brownie McGhee who were also embraced by the liberal New York City set. In an effort to broaden Lead Belly's appeal he recorded with the *a cappella* voices of the Golden Gate Quartet; it proved to be a somewhat contrived mismatch. Leadbelly also composed some new songs, one of which, 'Bourgeois Blues,' set to music some of the less than liberal prejudice he came across in Washington, D.C.

In 1949, Lead Belly visited Paris with a view to achieving what some of his contemporaries in the jazz field had done in building a white European following; it wasn't to be. His music seemed a little out of place to the left-bank crowd who always favored jazz over folk. Upon his return he was diagnosed with Lou Gehrig's disease, a sickness that destroys the muscular system; within a few months he was dead. Ironically, a year later The Weavers, the folk group led by Pete Seeger, recorded Lead Belly's 'Good Night Irene.' The song went to number 1 on *Billboard*'s pop charts. Seeger went on to write an instruction book and record an LP on Lead Belly's unique 12-string guitar technique. A few years later, Lonnie Donegan used Lead Belly's 'Rock Island Line' to launch the skiffle craze in Britain. Since then Lead Belly's influence has spread far beyond the folk arena; everyone from The Beach Boys to Led Zeppelin and Little Richard has covered him.

In 1988, Columbia Records released *Folkways: A Vision Shared*, on which Taj Mahal, Brian Wilson, Bruce Springsteen, Sweet Honey in the Rock, Bob Dylan, and John Mellencamp all sing Lead Belly and Woody Guthrie songs. The profits were used to purchase the Folkways Record catalog for the Smithsonian Institution.

Ironically, when he died he was virtually penniless, which is a sad indictment of those who

"He was one of the main movers when I was a kid." ~ *Robert Plant*

had sought to befriend him and use his talent to further their own careers and ambitions. How amazed he would have been that his songs would even top the charts, and his influence and legend would be acknowledged by so many… then again he might not. A proud man, and one who was not above a bit of self-promotion, he certainly believed in himself. If you can sing your way out of prison, making records and entertaining white audiences probably seems pretty easy.

"A Louisiana Legend."
~ The words on Lead Belly's gravestone

Lead Belly

BORN January c.1888 in Mooringsport, LA

DIED 6 December 1949 in New York, NY

INSTRUMENT Accordion, Bass, Guitar, Harmonica, Mandolin, Piano

FIRST RECORDED 1933

INFLUENCES Blind Lemon Jefferson

INFLUENCED Woody Guthrie, Lonnie Donegan, John Koerner, Sonny Terry & Brownie McGhee, Pete Seeger, Eric Burdon

CLASSIC TRACKS 'Goodnight Irene,' 'Rock Island Line,' 'C.C. Rider'

HEARING THE BLUES

The Minneapolis Private Party 1948 Document

Lead Belly's Last Session 1947 Smithsonian Folkways

Where Did You Sleep Last Night – Lead Belly's Legacy Vol. 1 Folkways

Bourgeois Blues – Lead Belly's Legacy Vol. 2 Folkways

R I

Rock Island

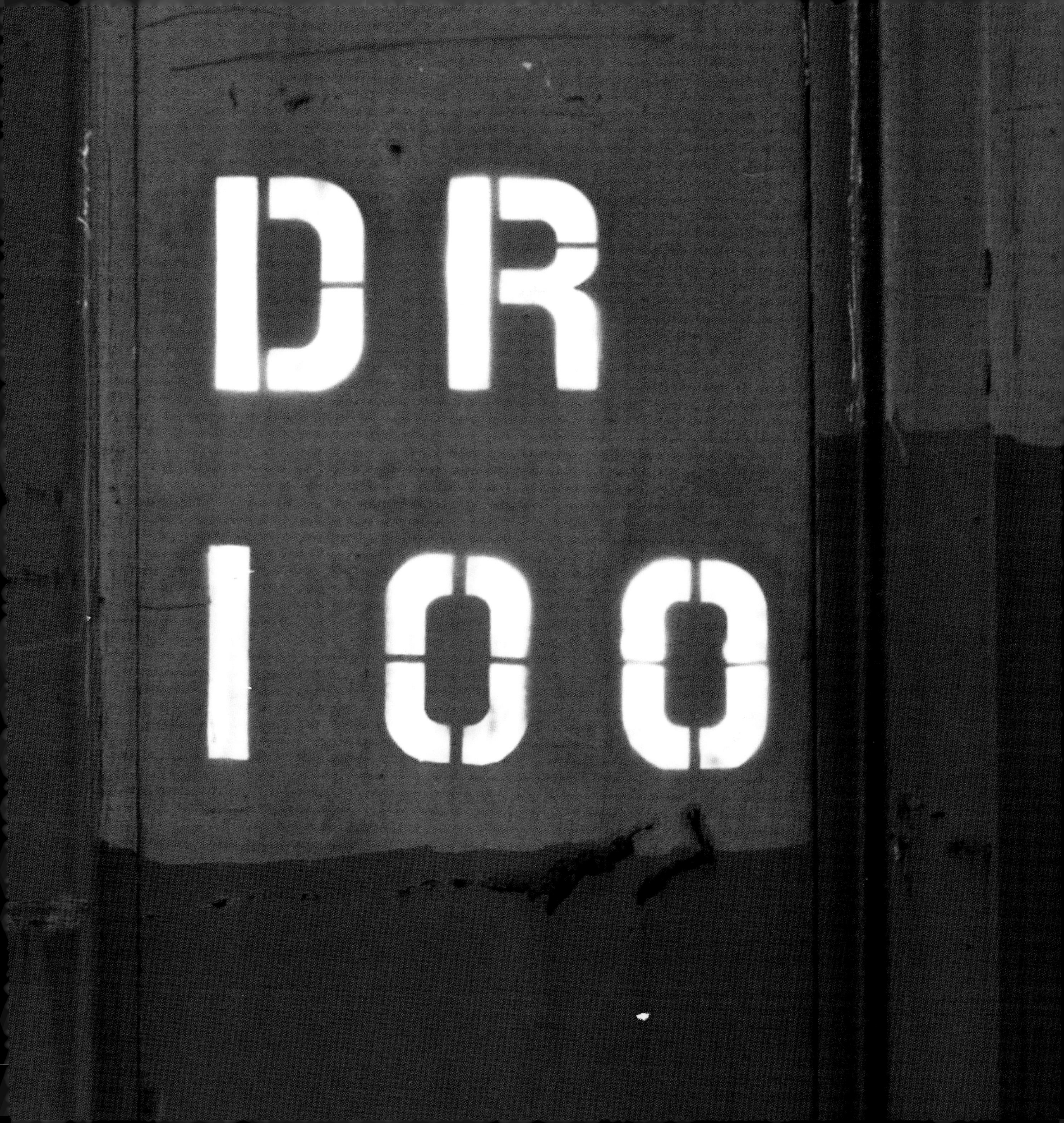
DR
100

Charley Patton

"Charley Patton is without question one of the most impressive and important of Bluesmen on record." ~ *Paul Oliver*

CHARLEY PATTON WAS a true Delta bluesman, maybe *the* Delta bluesman; his legend strides across the flat, parched landscape like no other musician of his generation. Already over 40 when he made first record he traveled extensively, which in some ways accounts for his influence. Stories about Patton all point to the fact that he was an original, a performer that many of the younger players held in high regard. But above all else Charley was an entertainer, which is precisely why he became so popular and so well remembered. Listen today to a poorly recorded, scratchy 78 and it's sometimes hard to accept that this man could have been so popular, and so very good.

Charley Patton was born in Edwards, Mississippi sometime around 1889, and his father was a preacher whose twelve children were raised on a farm. They later moved to Will Dockery's plantation when Charley was still a young boy, and it was there that he learned to play the guitar around 1908; he was 19 years old.

Many argue that Patton was the first great Mississippi bluesman, the fountainhead from which flowed the style that has come to be called Delta blues. His was a distinctive style, rampant and raw, yet rhythmic too. His vocal delivery was often hoarse, more of a holler than singing, often difficult to comprehend. He was one of the first to develop the slide guitar sound. Not only did Patton play the blues he lived them too. He was imprisoned, he drank heavily, had around eight wives and traveled extensively, which may have accounted for the number of wives. Nor was Patton someone who played the blues in a somber and laid-back fashion. He would often play his guitar behind his neck, and between his legs; he was a consummate showman.

"What he loved to do was clown with his guitar, just puttin' it all under his legs and back behind him." ~ *Sam Chatmon, Delta bluesman*

He learned from one of the earliest Delta blues players, a man named Henry Sloan, but no-one knows what he learned because Sloan never did get to record. By the time 5-feet-5-inch-tall Patton was in his mid-twenties he was known throughout the Delta, having played at picnics, juke joints, house parties as well as at levee camps. His friend Willie Brown often accompanied him; and the two of

"It was him who started me off to playing. He took a liking to me, and I asked him would he learn me." ~ *Howlin' Wolf*

them put on a real show. They often played for white audiences, especially in Lula, initially using Dockery Farms as their base. Patton's small frame housed an immensely loud voice, which was very useful given the lack of amplification, and it's said that he could be heard over 500 yards when he performed outdoors.

Charley Patton was 'discovered' by a 34-year-old Mississippi music-store owner and part-time record company scout by the name of Henry Speir. He contacted the Paramount Record Company and arranged for Patton to record in Richmond, Indiana on Friday 14 June 1929. He recorded 14 sides, probably the cream of his extensive repertoire at the time. The first record that Paramount released was

'Pony Blues' coupled with 'Banty Rooster Blues'; this one 78-rpm recording established Patton's reputation. His third Paramount release, 'Mississippi Bolweavil Blues' was credited to The Masked Marvel. Paramount asked record buyers to guess the artist on the record, their prize was another Paramount record of their choice... marketing 1920s style.

Charley was confident in his ability as a musician, and even got some people's backs up with his demands to be addressed as Mister Patton. Whether it was arrogance or confidence we can never know. He was a showman, of that there is no doubt, but it was also what was required of these entertainers, in no way should it undermine our view of Patton's musicianship or his status. It's clear from listening to his records that he was an original, he wrote wonderful songs and interesting lyrics; he also delivered them with a great deal more panache than just about any of his contemporaries. At least any of those that got to make a record; the lottery of the recorded blues could mean that there was someone better, it's just that they were never lucky enough to be put in front of a microphone. Records were only important for one reason. With no royalty payments they just helped to 'spread the word.' A player had to put on a show, and that's what Charley Patton did better than anyone.

About three months after his first session, Patton once again headed north, this time to Grafton, Wisconsin where he recorded another 22 sides for

Paramount, with Henry 'Son' Sims accompanying him on fiddle. At his third recording session in 1930 Willie Brown accompanied him; blues pianist Louise Johnson and Son House also went along for the ride and both ended up recording for Paramount. At this session Charley cut just four sides. It may have been that the cream of his material had been used up, and this was the 1920s equivalent of that difficult third album.

Many of Patton's recordings are tales of his own life, songs that many of his Delta audience could relate to, which was clearly a significant factor in his success. He also recorded topical songs that were, in their way, the news wire of the Delta. 'High Water Everywhere,' about the Mississippi flood of 1927, is one such. Given Patton's age he is the most likely performer, to be recorded, that truly reflects the genesis of the blues. He was there, absorbing and shaping the blues, as well as creating the opportunities for others to record. He was not the first country blues player to record, but he was by a long way the greatest of the early exponents of the blues.

With the onset of the Depression, Patton's recording career took a downturn and he did not record again until 1934, when he went to New York to cut some sides for Vocalion. He cut 36 sides over three days, ten of which were released at the time. These performances are not as good as Charley's

earlier work – he had a serious heart condition, a knife wound in his neck and he was just three months away from his death. His latest, and last, wife Bertha Lee accompanied him on some of these sides; sadly the masters of the unissued recordings are missing.

Patton and Bertha Lee left New York and went back to Mississippi. Three months later, on 28 April, the 43-year-old Patton died at Holly Springs near Indianola. At his last recording session he recorded the prophetic 'Oh Death':

Oh, hush, good Lordy, oh hush,
somebody is callin' me
Lord I know, Lord, I know my time ain't long.

Nearly 65 years later, his daughter Rosetta Patton recalled how she heard the news of her father's passing. "Well my stepfather came home and told me. I was sitting on the front porch rocking in a rocking chair and he said, 'Rosetta, I have something to tell you.' He said, 'Don't get upset, I have something to tell you.' And Momma, she rushed to the door, she said, 'What is it? What are you going to tell her?' He said, 'Her father's dead.' And I know that they say he had asthma and a heart attack. He went out to play that night, a Saturday night, he took a real sick attack and they rushed him home and he died before he got to the doctor back there."

"He was the loudest blues player I ever heard."
~ Sleepy John Estes

Charley Patton's daughter, Rosetta Patton

Charley Patton

BORN c1889 in Edwards (Hinds Co.)., MS

DIED 28 April 1934 in Indianola, MS

INSTRUMENT Guitar,

FIRST RECORDED 1929

INFLUENCES Henry Sloan, Lem Nichola

INFLUENCED Just about every Delta blues player, especially Son House, Muddy Waters, Robert Johnson, Howlin' Wolf

CLASSIC TRACKS 'Pony Blues,' 'High Water Everywhere,' 'A Spoonful Blues'

HEARING THE BLUES

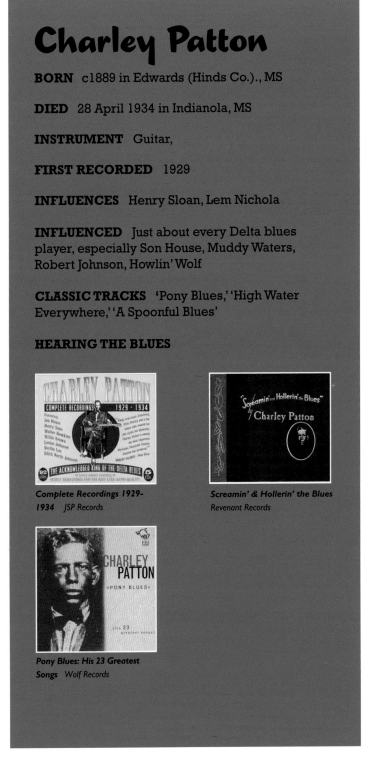

Complete Recordings 1929-1934 JSP Records

Screamin' & Hollerin' the Blues Revenant Records

Pony Blues: His 23 Greatest Songs Wolf Records

It is Patton's influence on many of the other artists that are now held in such high esteem that makes him even more important. Willie Brown, Son House, Howlin' Wolf, Tommy Johnson, Robert Johnson, Muddy Waters, Bukka White, Big Joe Williams, Pop Staples and David 'Honey Boy' Edwards all came under Patton's influence in some way. They may have played with him, known him as a friend, seen him perform or quite simply they aspired to be both as good and as well known as Patton. They took water from his well, allowing others who followed them to drink from their supply of the original Delta blues.

Blind Blake

"Blake was worthy of everything they said about him, he really was an artist."
~ Mayo Williams, Paramount Records

HE'S BEEN CALLED ragtime guitar's foremost fingerpicker and when you listen to his dexterous playing it's hard to argue. Beyond any other accolade granted to Blake he should be regarded as one of the best guitarists of his generation. He played fantastic ragtime guitar on numbers like 'Southern Rag' and 'Blind Arthur's Breakdown'; his talent led Paramount to use him on a number of sessions for other artists. Perhaps he should also be regarded as one of the original session guitarists. He was also the first man to use the 'rock' word on record.

The facts regarding Arthur Blake's birth date and early life are hard to unravel, even his real name is cloaked in mystery; it's most likely Arthur Phelps. 'Blake' was something of a nickname he acquired along the way; a 'blake' in the early part of the 20th century in the South was an unrelenting and tough character. It's thought that young Arthur, despite being born in Jacksonville, Florida, spent his youth in Georgia and began working as a street musician from a young age. He later worked throughout the South, playing for road gangs, at picnics and fish fries; like many other blind itinerant musicians he found work wherever he could.

He moved to Chicago in the early 1920s and probably began his recording career as an accompanist. After Art Laibly 'discovered' Blind Lemon Jefferson for Paramount there was pressure on other recording managers at the label to find black musicians, and especially blues musicians, who could appeal to the growing market, not only in the South but also Chicago and the other Northern cities to which people were migrating. Mayo Williams was Laiby's boss and he was the one that took Arthur Blake into the company's studio sometime during August 1926. His first record, 'West Coast Blues,' a ragtime number, backed by 'Early Morning Blues,' became a hit when it was released in October. It meant that within the space of six months Paramount had discovered two of the major stars of early blues.

Blake may also have been the first man to use the 'rock' word in a song; he certainly was the first to have a record that mentions it. 'West Coast Blues' opens with the lines "Now we gonna do the old

"His voice was quiet, slightly wistful, giving his blues the feeling of self-deprecating irony." *~ Giles Oakley,* The Devil's Music: A History of the Blues, *BBC TV, 1976*

"Blind Blake, a very good guitar player, about the best for my money." ~ *Josh White*

country rock. First thing we do, swing your partners." Later in the song he even does a little advertising: "Good to the last drop, just like Maxwell House coffee, yes." When President Theodore Roosevelt visited the Maxwell House Coffee manufacturing plant in 1907 he had a cup of their coffee and when he finished it he said, "It's good to the last drop." The company cleverly adopted it as their slogan and it's therefore the only known example of a U.S. president being an advertising copywriter.

Between his debut and 1932 he recorded over 80 solo titles for

Paramount, which gives some idea of his popularity. No record company would invest time and money in an artist who wasn't selling, as can be evidenced by the fact that many of the early bluesmen recorded just a handful of sides. Some of his releases came out under different names. These included Blind George Martin, Blind Arthur, Billy James and best of all, and somewhat bizarrely, Gorgeous Weed and Stinking Socks! Among the artists that he is known to have accompanied on record are Ma Rainey, Leola Wilson, Irene Scruggs and Papa Charlie Jackson; he also recorded a memorable duet, 'Hastings Street,' with Charlie Spand. In 1930 he toured with a small band and appeared in a show called *Happy Go Lucky*.

In 1929, Blind Blake and other Paramount recording artists made what has been described as the first sampler record when the Paramount All Stars recorded *Home Town Skiffle*. The record label credits Blind Lemon Jefferson, Blind Blake, Will Ezell, Charlie Spand, Papa Charlie Jackson and the Hokum Boys; The Hokum Boys were made up of the others plus Alex Hill and Georgia Tom Dorsey. The record has one or two choruses of a number of the artists' best-known records. It is also the first known mention of 'skiffle.' In Britain,

"I met Blind Blakes (sic) in Chicago. I couldn't second him. He was too fast for me." ~ *Ishman Bracey, Mississippi bluesman*

skiffle had a profound effect on rock music in the late 1950s and early 1960s, influencing, though Lonnie Donegan, everyone from The Beatles to The Rolling Stones, The Who and just about every band who came along during the 'Beat Boom.'

Many of Blake's records were characterized by incorporating ragtime and jazz into the blues. There are some who say he should not be labeled as a blues artist, given that he recorded old-style ballads and vaudeville numbers, however he did record many straight blues tunes. He was one of the most popular blues recording artists of the 1920s. His success was in part responsible for record companies seeking out other country blues players to record. Blake's playing was responsible for many people latching onto the idea of playing a riff, and for many years few could match his mastery. It was through listening to his records that many young blues players in the 1930s were inspired to learn their craft.

The precise circumstances of his death are unknown, as is the date. It is likely that he died soon after the demise of Paramount Records in the early 30s. Rumours of his demise, often circulated by other musicians, range from him being run down by a streetcar to death from drinking moonshine. His influence lived on in the work of other bluesmen from the East, including Blind Boy Fuller.

Blind Blake

BORN Probably in Jacksonville, FL c1890-1895

DIED c1933 in Florida

INSTRUMENT Guitar

FIRST RECORDED 1926

INFLUENCED Blind Boy Fuller, Big Bill Broonzy, Josh White

CLASSIC TRACKS 'Blind Arthur's Breakdown,' 'West Coast Blues,' 'Hastings Street'

HEARING THE BLUES

All The Published Sides
JSP Records

The Best of Blind Blake
Yazoo

Big Bill Broonzy

"Big Bill – that's the nicest guy I ever met in my life." ~ *Muddy Waters*

BIG BILL BROONZY was a giant of the 1930s urban blues scene, a key player in the transition between the country blues of the Mississippi Delta and the electric blues of 1950s Chicago. Born in Mississippi and raised in Arkansas, he took what he knew from the Delta blues and imbued it with urban sophistication; in so doing he became one of the dominant bluesmen of the pre-war Chicago blues scene. His influence was huge, both through his music and his personality, which like him was BIG.

"When I was about ten years old, I made a fiddle out of a cigar box, a guitar out of goods boxes for my buddy Louis Carter, and we would play for the white people's picnics." ~ *Big Bill Broonzy*

William Lee Conley Broonzy was one of 17 children whose parents had been born into slavery. He grew up in Pine Bluffs, Arkansas with an interest in music from a young age and by his mid-teens he was playing the fiddle at country parties while working as a farmhand. By the time he was 19 years old he was an itinerant preacher. Following this he served for two years in the U.S. Army. In 1920 he moved to Chicago to find regular work, and at night he played part-time with Papa Charlie Jackson. In August 1924, Jackson was one of the first country blues artists to record when Paramount took him into a Chicago studio to cut 'Papa's Lawdy Lawdy Blues' and 'Airy Man Blues.' It was around the same time that Broonzy learned to play the guitar.

Big Bill, as he was dubbed on his first record for the Paramount label, was aptly named as he was a big man; he was also by all accounts a good man. It was November 1927 when he cut 'House Rent Stomp' under the name of Big Bill and Thomps. He recorded several more cuts under the same name. but by 1930 he was recording for the Perfect label as Sammy Sampson. In 1959 George Jones, the country singer, had a hit on the U.S. Country charts called 'Who Shot Sam.' "I met Sammy Sampson down in New Orleans. He had a lot of money, and a big limousine. He took me honky-tonking on Saturday night." Could it be that George Jones met Big Bill?

Throughout the 1930s he was a prolific recording artist – perhaps the most prolific. He recorded on a variety of labels as Big Bill Johnson, Big Bill Broomsley, Big Bill and his Jug Busters, Big Bill and his Orchestra, Big Bill and The Memphis Five and

"Blues is a natural fact, something that a fellow lives. If you don't live it, you don't have it." ~ *Big Bill Broonzy*

just plain Big Bill. Part of Broonzy's attraction to the blacks that had migrated to the cities was his singing about things that mattered to them. He gave country matters an urban tinge. In 1936 he recorded 'WPA Blues,' which is a great example of the immediacy of the blues to talk about subjects important to its audience, as well as of Broonzy having his finger on the pulse of black interest. In the wake of President Roosevelt's New Deal, the Works Project Administration (WPA) was set up to provide work for laborers as well as writers and artists. This federal relief program attracted many thousands of out-of-work blacks and whites between 1935 and 1939.

In 1938 and 1939 he appeared on the stage of Carnegie Hall in New York in John Hammond's *Spirituals to Swing Concert* with other major blues and jazz artists; he was introduced as a Mississippi plow-hand. "William 'Big Bill' Broonzy bought a new pair of shoes and got on a bus in Arkansas to make his first trip to New York," wrote John Sabastian in a review that appeared in *New Masses*. It was his first trip, if you ignore the eight days of recording on three separate sessions in 1930 and 1932! It was all part of the pre-war romanticizing of the blues by some sections of New York society.

Besides being a prodigious solo recording artist Broonzy was a hard-working accompanist. He worked with Jazz Gillum, Washboard Sam (Sam was his cousin), Memphis Minnie, Tampa Red, John Lee (Sonny Boy) Williamson, Lonnie Johnson, Lil Green, Cripple Clarence Lofton, and Victoria Spivey. He also had a simultaneous recording career as part of The Famous Hokum Boys and The Hokum Boys. He

was a prolific songwriter with a knack of writing songs that appealed to his more sophisticated city audience, as well as people that shared his country roots. The broad sweep of his repertoire helped in establishing Bill's reputation and appeal. He performed across a wider musical spectrum than almost any other bluesman before or since. He played ragtime, hokum blues, straight-ahead country blues, sophisticated city blues, jazz-tinged songs, folk songs and spirituals.

Folk Singers Tour Colleges

Chicago—Four men who've integrated three highly different varieties of folk music in an unusual concert program are, from the left, Studs Terkel, Win Stracke, Big Bill Broonzy, and Lawrence Lane. Terkel, who juggles a career embracing writing, acting, and disc jockeying, acts as narrator. Stracke sings the songs of the American pioneer and laboring man; Broonzy sings the blues, and Lane, like Stracke a highly trained concert singer, specializes in Elizabethan songs and ballads. Story on the group in next column.

Big Bill Broonzy also claims the credit for introducing Tommy McClennan to Lester Melrose at Bluebird. In late 1939 McClennan recorded 'Bottle It Up and Go,' which highlights the widening gap

"'Guitar Shuffle' was one of the first tracks I learnt to play, but even to this day I can't play it exactly right." ~ *Ronnie Wood of The Rolling Stones*

between city and rural black communities, and not just in their choice of music. Broonzy recounts, in his autobiography, how he was there when Tommy recorded 'Bottle It Up and Go.' Broonzy advised against using 'nigger' in the lyric. "You're gonna get in trouble with that song." "I'll never change my song," was Tommy's response. Soon after, Tommy played the song at a party in the city, and it went over very badly. Tommy was forced to make a speedy exit through a window and he and Big Bill had to run all the way to a friend's house.

After World War II, Broonzy recorded songs that were the bridge that allowed many younger musicians to cross over to the future of the blues: the electric blues of post-war Chicago. His 1945 recordings of 'Where the Blues Began,' with Big Maceo on piano and Buster Bennett on sax, or 'Martha Blues' with Memphis Slim on piano, clearly show the way forward.

"Big Bill had been around a long time in Chicago when I come up in '43 so he helped me get my start."
~ *Muddy Waters*

Cut a slice through any year of the 1930s and there's Bill Broonzy, like the writing through a stick of seaside rock. He was a mentor, performer, and inspirational figure and the man who was, perhaps,

more responsible than any other for taking the blues to Britain and Europe. As the self-proclaimed 'last of his line' he wooed the young Turks of the European jazz scene. In their desire to understand and learn about the blues they took Bill to their hearts. If Bill played it, it was good, acceptable and most of all it was genuine. In 1951 he toured Britain and Europe, the following year he visited with the pianist Blind John Davis. Later still he traveled again to Britain with Brother John Sellers, as well as the white folk-blues player Ramblin' Jack Elliott. For European audiences his clear diction and abilities as a raconteur made him the perfect ambassador for the blues.

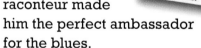

With the arrival of post-war electric blues and artists that included Muddy Waters, who had great respect for Bill, Broonzy simply reinvented himself. He became what is best described as a folk-blues artist, demonstrating how the two forms are so closely linked. Nevertheless, Broonzy, like almost all of his contemporaries, still needed to work outside music to support himself. He worked as a janitor in the early 50s at Iowa State University, which is where some of the students taught him to write. This new skill allowed him to collaborate in the writing of his biography with Yannick Bruynoghe, which further established Broonzy's reputation. In 1956 he was diagnosed with throat cancer, which often made performing very painful. It did not stop him, and on 12 July 1957 he went into the studio to record a unique 'last will and testament,' a five-LP boxed set that was released on Verve. Entitled *The Bill Broonzy Story,* this was Broonzy at his best, telling the stories behind the songs, vignettes from his own life and taking an extensive saunter through his vast repertoire: he was second only to Leadbelly in the number of songs that he knew.

Broonzy died on 15 August 1958, and at his funeral his friends turned out in force. They included Tampa Red, Muddy Waters, Mahalia Jackson, Sunnyland Slim and J.B. Lenoir. The Broonzy legend has dimmed somewhat since his death, and it is as though his popularity was his undoing; sometimes obscurity serves a reputation better.

"Big Bill was different. He always did have a modest way about him – he never did raise his voice in any way."
~ Brother John Sellers

Big Bill Broonzy

BORN 26 June 1893 in Scott, Bolivar Co., MS

DIED 15 August 1958 in Chicago, IL

INSTRUMENT Guitar, Mandolin, Fiddle

FIRST RECORDED 1927

INFLUENCES Papa Charlie Jackson, Blind Lemon Jefferson, Lonnie Johnson, Peatie Wheatstraw

INFLUENCED J.B. Lenoir, Muddy Waters, Brownie McGhee, Memphis Slim, Jimmy Witherspoon, Keith Richards

CLASSIC TRACKS 'Key To The Highway,' 'Southbound Train'

HEARING THE BLUES

The Bill Broonzy Story Verve

All The Classic Sides 1928–1937 JSP Records

An Introduction To Big Bill Broonzy Fuel

Big Bill Broonzy 1937–1940 JSP Records

Bessie Smith

"Bessie Smith was destined to be the greatest Negro recording artist of her day and one of the most outstanding figures in the whole history of American music." ~ *Paul Oliver*

BESSIE SMITH WAS MUCH MORE than just a blues singer; she was an icon for her race. She lived her life with the needle permanently in the red, combining drinking, fighting and sex with both men and women. Years of working the vaudeville circuit honed Bessie's skills as a powerful singer and entertainer, and along the way she became an established star with black audiences, especially when she sang live, belting out her songs, never needing a microphone. Bessie Smith sang the life she lived.

The woman who became known as the 'Empress of the Blues' was one of seven children born in 1894 in Chattanooga, Tennessee to a part-time Baptist preacher and his wife; by the time she was nine years old both her parents were dead, by which time Bessie and her brother Andrew were singing on the streets of Chattanooga for spare change, while their brother Clarence, a comedian and dancer, joined a travelling vaudeville show. In 1912, Clarence arranged an audition with the Moses Stokes Company for his 18-year-old sister, and joining as a dancer she eventually became a featured singer. The star of the company was Ma Rainey, which has given rise to the debate as to whether or not Ma coached young Bessie in her vocal skills. She may have actively done so; it is

certainly inconceivable that the younger singer would not have looked up to the 26 year old 'star' and not picked up a thing or two.

In 1921, having already been married and widowed, Bessie Smith moved to Philadelphia, well aware of her namesake Mamie Smith's success with 'Crazy Blues,' the first recorded blues song. In order to get her own recording career underway, Bessie auditioned for Okeh Records, but her recording of 'I Wish I Could Shimmy Like My Sister Kate' was deemed not worthy of a release; more auditions followed, all ended in rejection.

Then on a Thursday, the day after Valentine's Day, in 1923, with Clarence Williams on the piano, the 28-year-old Bessie Smith cut '"Tain't Nobody's Business If I Do' and 'Down Hearted Blues'; the latter song was a cover of a two-year-old hit by Alberta Hunter. The session was not quite right, so next day Bessie and Clarence were back again. This time they re-did 'Down Hearted Blues' and recorded 'Gulf Coast Blues,' a song written by Williams.

Anyone privileged to be at the session would have been struck by Bessie Smith's self-assured phrasing, as well as the power of her delivery honed from years of singing without a microphone on the vaudeville circuit. Standing around six feet

"She was a difficult and temperamental person, she had her love affairs, which frequently interfered with her work, but she never was a real problem. Bessie was a person for whose artistry, at least, I had the profoundest respect." ~ *Frank Schiffman, owner of the Apollo Theater, Harlem, New York*

tall and weighing nearly 200 pounds, it was not difficult to work out from where her power emanated. By June of 1923 Bessie Smith was a star; 'Down Hearted Blues' was effectively the number one song in America, although this was in the days before proper hit record charts. Black Swan, one of the labels who rejected Bessie, were probably kicking themselves; they thought her voice 'a little too rough.'

In 1923 Bessie met and married Jack Gee. He was an illiterate night-watchman, but was instrumental in helping Bessie sort out her business affairs. Clarence Williams, who had been pivotal in securing Bessie's Columbia contract, was acting as much on his own behalf as the singer's. Bessie signed a contract that she thought was with Columbia, whereas in fact she was signing an exclusive management deal with Mr. Williams; it gave him 50% of Bessie's record earnings. When Bessie found out, she and Gee made a surprise visit to Clarence Williams' office and secured a release from the old deal, enabling her to sign directly with Columbia. The new contract gave Bessie $200 per issued side, whereas she had got just $125 from the Williams contract, although she still earned no royalties from her recordings. For Bessie, her records were a way of promoting her live performances; as she is reported to have earned around $2,000 per week from personal appearances, it certainly worked. Reports vary as to how many copies of 'Down Hearted Blues' actually sold, but at the top end is two million, which meant that if she had have accepted royalties then she would have made even more money.

"I sang blues – Bessie Smith kind of blues. No one ever hit me so hard... Bessie made me want to sing." ~ *Janis Joplin*

"So by the end of high school I was listening to Bessie Smith and Leadbelly." ~ *Maria Muldaur*

Bessie was one of the most prolific recording artists of her era; from 1923 to 1933 she recorded in excess of 150 songs for Columbia. In April 1923, at the third session, she finally recorded a version of ''Tain't Nobody's Business If I Do' that Columbia felt was worth releasing, and what a release; it became a classic. While many of her earlier recordings were just Bessie's powerful voice and a piano accompaniment, she later worked with small groups that included many of the finest musicians of the period, including pianists Fletcher Henderson and James P. Johnson, saxophonist Coleman Hawkins, and future jazz legend Louis Armstrong. In 1929, Smith recorded what might well be regarded as her 'personal epitaph,' 'Nobody Knows You When You're Down and Out.' It was also in 1929 that she made her only film appearance, with James P. Johnson, in *St Louis Blues*. Two years later Columbia dropped her from their roster; it was virtually the end of Bessie's recording career. She recorded her last four sides in November 1933, these were for Okeh; it was a date arranged by the legendary producer John Hammond, who would later sign Bob Dylan among many others.

In 1934 she was in a touring show and in 1935 she appeared, to critical acclaim, at the Apollo Theater in New York. Bessie's last New York appearance was on a cold February Sunday afternoon in 1936 at the original Famous Door on 52nd Street. At the time, much was made of the fact that Mildred Bailey refused to follow Bessie's

performance. The difficulty for Bessie, a difficulty that many who followed her have also discovered, is that people's tastes change; her style had become out of date, the record-buying public were looking for something new and more sophisticated. Nevertheless she remained a good draw on the live circuit.

On 26 September 1937, the day before John Hammond was to leave for Mississippi to take Bessie back to New York to record, she and her lover Richard Morgan (jazz man Lionel Hampton's uncle) were driving on Route 61 in Coahoma County, just north of Clarksdale, Mississippi, when their car, which Morgan was driving, had an accident. It is thought that he was following the telephone poles that were being lit by the moonlight. Unfortunately he did not realize that the poles crossed over the road as it turned sharply to the right. As a result their car ran off the road and down a steep embankment created by the Yazoo flood-plain. Bessie broke her ribs in the crash and as she lay by the side of the road, being treated, a truck ran over her right arm, nearly severing it.

For many years the rumor circulated that her life could have been saved, if she had not been refused treatment at a 'whites-only' hospital in Clarksdale, which was 14 miles from the crash site. Much of the 'blame' for this erroneous story must be attributed to John Hammond. He wrote an article in *Down Beat* magazine claiming Bessie died after being denied admission to a hospital because of her skin color;

Hammond has since admitted his article was based on hearsay. Bessie was in fact treated by a white doctor, Dr. Hugh Smith, at the blacks-only hospital on Sunflower Avenue in Clarksdale.

The building is now a hotel called The Riverside. The room in which Bessie died of her internal injuries has always been kept unlet, as a shrine to her memory. It's all grist to the myth-making mill that has been created around Bessie Smith – a woman whose legend has done much to inspire others to follow her as a blues singer, and a character who was larger than life.

"I've been poor and I've been rich, and rich is better."
~ *Bessie Smith*

Bessie Smith

BORN 15 April 1894 in Chattanooga, TN

DIED 26 September 1937 in Clarksdale, MS

INSTRUMENT Vocalist

FIRST RECORDED 1923

INFLUENCES Ma Rainey

INFLUENCED Billie Holiday, Mahalia Jackson, Odetta, Victoria Spivey, Big Mama Thornton, Dinah Washington, Janis Joplin

CLASSIC TRACKS ''Tain't Nobody's Business If I Do,' 'Mama's Got The Blues,' 'Backwater Blues,' 'Nobody Knows You When You're Down And Out'

HEARING THE BLUES

The Essential Bessie Smith
Sony

The Greatest Blues Singer In The World   Blues Encore

Empress of the Blues 1926-1933
JSP Records Box Set

Blind Lemon Jefferson

"Can anyone imagine a fate more horrible than to find that one is blind?... Such was the fate of Blind Lemon Jefferson... He learned to play a guitar, and for years he entertained his friends freely – moaning his weird songs as a means of forgetting his affliction."

~ *The Paramount Book of the Blues, 1927*

NO ONE KNOWS FOR SURE if Lemon was his real name, but there is no doubt that his name resonates as an early giant of country blues music. Blind Lemon's delivery, his unusual phrasing and the way he combined his guitar and vocals to enhance the melody line was what made him unique. His material was also brilliant and when combined with his unusual delivery it made him almost impossible to copy. It meant that for the first time the artist was pre-eminent: Lemon produced 'a sound,' something that stood him apart from other artists. The artist was now the star, not the material, added to which Blind Lemon Jefferson became a pop star. It also meant that for the first time a man dominated the blues.

Born blind on a farm in east Texas in 1897, he was one of seven children and probably learned to play guitar to eke out a living. By the time he was 20 he was performing at house parties and soon after moved to Dallas where he played on street corners. He was obviously good as he was soon earning enough to support both a wife and a child; some have written that he could earn $150 on a good day, which may be fanciful, but it gives some idea of his talent. Although he is known as a bluesman he, like many of his contemporaries, also sang spirituals and folk tunes, it was important to be able to play what the people wanted if you needed to earn your living. There is little doubt that Jefferson traveled extensively before he took up recording, which goes some way to explaining the wide variety of his material.

Jefferson could well have stayed on street corners but for the foresight of R.T. Ashford, a Dallas storeowner, who sold Paramount's records in his shop; he contacted Art Laibly, Paramount's

"When I was boy, I think the first blues record I ever heard was Blind Lemon Jefferson singing 'Black Snake Moan.'"
~ Mississippi Fred McDowell

marketing director, suggesting he record the 27-year-old Blind Lemon. Ashford's approach to Paramount was nothing out of the ordinary, neither was he motivated out of kindness for Blind Lemon, he saw it as an opportunity to make money. It was obvious that Jefferson was popular around Dallas and Ashford saw the chance of selling records to Lemon's local fans. Paramount agreed to record Jefferson and sometime in December 1925 or January 1926 he was taken to Chicago. For some strange reason either Blind Lemon or Paramount was not keen on him singing the blues; he recorded two spirituals before heading home to Dallas. These first recordings were released a few months later under the name Deacon L.J. Bates; there would be other recordings over the next few years as Deacon Bates. A couple of months later he was back in Chicago. This time he did record four blues sides, including what became the first of his records to be released under his own name – 'Long Lonesome Blues.' Paramount could not have anticipated the result. 'Long Lonesome Blues' came

out in May, Paramount and Blind Lemon changed forever the face of recorded blues… and arguably the course of popular music.

Rival record companies were used to producing cover versions, on which their own stars replicated other artists' records; they were then able to take a share of the sales. Jefferson's popularity meant that other record companies realized that their Southern audiences were anxious to hear performers who were like the ones that they were used to listening to; not quasi blues performers from an older tradition. Some labels arranged for their field recording units to visit the South in the search for new talent. These visits became more frequent and other labels were soon combing the countryside for new talent.

Meanwhile, Paramount quickly recorded more Blind Lemon Jefferson material. He cut 'Jack O'Diamonds Blues' in May and followed it with 11 more sides by the end of 1926. In March 1927,

"And then there was a Texas-born blues singer called Lemon Jefferson. So that was the second one that I liked so much."
~ B.B. King

BLIND Lemon Jefferson added a wonderful hit to his long list of Blind Lemon Blues when he sang "Rabbit Food Blues". A great accompaniment, too, on his guitar.

Jefferson was back in the studio for what was a busy and productive day. This time he was not in Chicago but in Atlanta and he was recording for Okeh not Paramount; recording contracts back then were not quite so binding. He recorded two blues classics for Okeh, 'Black Snake Moan' and 'Matchbox Blues'; they were released on one record. 'Matchbox Blues' is typically Jefferson; it features simultaneous single-string picking and repeated bass lines.

Paramount quickly got Blind Lemon back into their studio cutting a version of 'Matchbox Blues' for his original label to release. He cut another 18 sides for Paramount by the end of 1927, including the immortal 'See That My Grave is Kept Clean.' In 1928 he did 24 more songs, followed by 14 in the first 8 months of 1929 before going to Richmond to cut his final 12 sides on Tuesday 24 September. His massive record sales afforded him the luxury of two cars and a chauffeur.

Three months later this giant of the blues was dead. He had either frozen to death in the snow, or had a heart attack after leaving a club in Chicago. He was found dead in the street the next morning, covered in snow; his guitar lay by his side. Between 1926 and 1929 he cut over 90 sides, making him the most recorded of the early bluesmen.

Blind Lemon Jefferson

BORN 11 july 1897 in Couchman (Freestone Co.), TX

DIED December 1929 in Chicago, IL

INSTRUMENT Guitar

FIRST RECORDED 1925

INFLUENCED T-Bone Walker, B.B. King, Lightnin' Hopkins, Rev. Gary Davis, Lead Belly

CLASSIC TRACKS 'Matchbox Blues,' 'See That My Grave Is Kept Clean,' 'Outside Woman Blues'

HEARING THE BLUES

The Best of Blind Lemon Jefferson   Yazoo

Classic Sides
JSP Records Box Set

Black Snake Moan   Snapper

Memphis Minnie

"She was a very funny woman and she always wore those great big ear-rings... and she was a very fine guitarist... Big Bill would never do anything unless'n he called Minnie."
~ Brother John Sellers

WOMEN HAVE A prominent place in early blues history, but by the early 1930s their popularity on record had begun to wane as the bluesmen from the Delta began serving up exactly what the public wanted. However, in Memphis Minnie even the best bluesmen had a competitor who was well able to beat most of them at their own game. She was a late starter, being already 32 years old when she first recorded, but her career would go on to span three decades and it was Minnie that kept the female blues flame burning brightly in an increasingly male-dominated era.

Minnie was born Lizzie Douglas in Algiers, Louisiana in 1897, and despite being the oldest of 13 brothers and sisters she was known to her family as 'Kid.' She grew up about 20 miles from Memphis and began playing guitar with Willie Brown when she was around 18 years old at parties and dances in and around Bedford, Mississippi. There's even talk of her joining the circus, but by the early 1920s she had settled in Memphis and lived with and may have even married a man named Will Weldon, although no one is quite sure. Blues historians have claimed that Will was married to Memphis Minnie in the 1920s, and this was the same man that recorded

with her and others, as well as solo, in the mid-1930s; by which time they claim he was calling himself Casey Bill Welson. An excellent book by Paul and Beth Garon entitled *Woman with Guitar – Memphis Minnie's Blues* questions this theory.

While we have no evidence, we would side with the Garons, Will Weldon was not Casey Bill Weldon who recorded with Peetie Wheatstraw in 1935. Minnie worked for tips, playing on Beale Street, and later joined Jed Davenport's Beale Street Jug Band. By 1929, she had married Joe McCoy, a good singer and guitarist, and together they played in a Beale street barbershop. One day a Columbia Records scout spotted them there and

"Acknowledged by her contemporaries among blues singers as the greatest of the women singers outside the classic vein." *~ Paul Oliver*

"She was a guitar king." ~ *Willie Brown*

offered to take them to New York to make some records. The haunting 'Bumble Bee Blues' was their 'hit' from that first session and over the years Minnie remade it for a number of different labels.

It was Columbia that renamed her Memphis Minnie, probably because they liked the way it sounded alongside Kansas Joe McCoy.

Among the many sides recorded in 1929 was their composition written about the Great Mississippi Flood of 1927 entitled 'When The Levee Breaks,' to be covered 43 years later by Led Zeppelin and appearing on their 1971 album *Led Zeppelin IV*.

Minnie, unlike many of her male counterparts, was quick to embrace the latest technology in order to be heard above the crowds. She took up the National guitar in 1929, one of the first blues players to do so, and she played an electric wood-body National as well as other electric guitars in the late 1930s and early 1940s. By 1933 Minnie had moved to

Chicago, and there was a legendary guitar-cutting contest between her and Big Bill Broonzy at which she played 'Me and My Chauffeur Blues' and 'Looking the World Over.' Minnie won the prize of a bottle of whiskey.

Minnie was a regular in the Chicago clubs, in particular the DeLisa and the Music Box. But her marriage, and naturally her musical partnership, with Joe McCoy ended in the mid-1930s. Minnie from then on was increasingly featured as a guitarist and vocalist, usually on material she had written. Her style was rooted in the country but flowered in the vibrant pre-war Chicago music scene, which is where she recorded the majority of over one hundred pre-war releases. She worked with a whole host of excellent blues performers, which bears testament to her talent.

Among those that she recorded with, besides Joe McCoy, were the Jed Devenport Jug Band, Georgia Tom, Tampa Red, Black Bob, Blind John Davis and Little Son Joe. She also sat in with Bumble Bee Slim and the Memphis Jug Band. Ironically, given her relationship with Will Weldon in Memphis in the 1920s, it was in Chicago in the

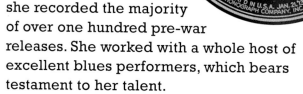

"The best thing goin' in the woman line." ~ *Bukka White*

Memphis Minnie and Kansas Joe McCoy

"A musical version of electric welders plus a rolling mill." ~ *The poet Langton Hughes describing Minnie's guitar playing in 1942*

mid-1930s that Minnie also recorded with Casey Bill Weldon. She also worked live with Big Bill Broonzy, who became her friend after their cutting contest, Sunnyland Slim and Roosevelt Sykes. By the late 1930s Minnie had married Little Son Joe and their relationship was to last for the next two decades.

Minnie used her electric guitar to good effect on her biggest hit, 'Me and My Chauffeur Blues,' recorded in 1941 with Little Son. The song, which used the same tune as 'Good Morning Little Schoolgirl,' became influential to many that heard it. Koko Taylor said, "It was the first blues record I ever heard." Lightnin' Hopkins even 'answered' Minnie with his 1960 song 'Automobile Blues.' Chuck Berry based his 'I Want To Be Your Driver' on Minnie's record, while Jefferson Airplane adapted it as 'Chauffeur Blues' on their 1966 debut album. Unfortunately Jefferson Airplane neglected to acknowledge Minnie's recording and failed to pay any royalties as a result.

The longevity of Minnie's career meant that her records cover a wide range of subject matter. Many of her songs, like 'Bumble Bee,' 'Dirty Mother For You' and 'Butcher Man,' were openly sexual; all were delivered in her confident open style. Others like 'Ma Rainey' and

'He's in the Ring (Doing That Same Old Thing)' were about celebrities. 'Ma Rainey' was recorded just six months after her death, while her unusual boxing tribute in 1935 was for Joe Louis. Minnie also tackled crime, voodoo, trains, health, and the perennial blues subject of chickens! Minnie constantly toured and played juke joints and fish fries, which certainly helped in maintaining her popularity. She stayed in touch with her audience, singing about what they both knew, and understood.

The lady who was at the forefront of transforming the blues into 'pop music' continued to record up until 1954. By then her health was failing, so both she and Little Son Joe retired to live in Memphis. Little Son died in 1961 and soon after the woman who was remembered by many of her musical contemporaries from Chicago as a hard-drinking woman had a stroke. Her sister looked after her for a while before she moved Minne into a nursing home. Despite her huge popularity and considerable record sales Minnie had little or no money, but after various magazines printed appeals fans began sending her donations. Among those that went to her aid was Jo Ann Kelly, the British blues singer who recorded in the late 1960s and 70s and always claimed Memphis Minnie as an inspiration.

She and her brother raised money for Minnie at a blues club benefit and arranged for a Memphian blues fan to deliver it to her in the nursing home. Minnie died on 6 August 1973.

"The hundreds of sides Minnie recorded are the perfect material to teach us about the blues. For the blues are at once general, and particular, speaking for millions, but in a highly singular, individual voice. Listening to Minnie's songs we hear her fantasies, her dreams, her desires, but we will hear them as if they were our own."
~ The words on Memphis Minnie's gravestone

Memphis Minnie

BORN 3 June 1897 in Algiers, LA

DIED 6 August 1973 in Memphis, TN

INSTRUMENT Guitar, Banjo

FIRST RECORDED 1929

INFLUENCES Jim McCoy, Frank Stokes

INFLUENCED Jo Ann Kelly, Maria Muldaur, Big Mama Thornton

CLASSIC TRACKS 'Me And My Chauffeur Blues,' 'I Am Sailin',' 'Bumble Bee,' 'You Got To Get Out Of Here'

HEARING THE BLUES

Queen of Country Blues 1929-1937 JSP Records

Hoodoo Lady
Snapper

Columbia Original Masters
Sony / BMG

Early Rhythm & Blues From The 1948 Regal Sessions
Collectables

PUMPER
No. 4

RED BA

V.F.

MARSHA

NKS

L CO.

Sonny Boy Williamson

"He did not give away all his secrets either in conversation or music. Instead, when he played, he built up the tension of his phrasing with logical development. One had to listen for quite a while as he progressed from short bursts, single notes, punctuated phrases to filigree patterns of complexity and richness." ~ *Paul Oliver*

THROUGHOUT HIS LIFE he was the master of misinformation and so details of his young life are both sketchy and confusing, and for that matter almost every period of his life. An inveterate liar, he even maintained that he was the original Sonny Boy Williamson, rather than the original whose name was John Lee Williamson who recorded two decades earlier. His own liberal way with the truth, and his desire to confuse and confound, should in no way detract from his talent. He was a giant, not just of the harmonica, but also as a composer and performer. Sonny Boy commanded attention on stage, and it is clear that he had a presence even larger than his six-foot wiry frame. Quite simply, he was one of the most charismatic performers in the whole blues genre.

Like the man whose name he took, the original Sonny Boy Williamson, Sonny Boy No.2, did much to shape the harmonica's place in the story of the blues. He was born Aleck Ford in Glendora, Mississippi, possibly, in 1899, and was the illegitimate son of Millie Ford, but he later took his stepfather's name – Miller. Such is the confusion about Sonny Boy's early life that his gravestone gives his birthday as 11 March 1897, while others have argued he was born in 1910! Whatever the truth, he began playing when he was just five years old and quickly developed into an accomplished harmonica player. From a young age he earned tips from playing street corners, dances and house rent parties. As he hoboed around the South he used the name Little Boy Blue, which is who Mick

"We used to call him Little Boy Blue. He had a belt with all his harmonicas in, and used to wear it round his waist. That was around 1932." ~ *Homesick James*

Jagger and Keith Richards named their first band after in 1961 – Little Boy Blue & The Blue Boys.

Sometime in the 1930s, Sonny Boy married Mary Burnett, Howlin' Wolf's half-sister; during this period he taught his young half-brother-in-law the harmonica. Sonny Boy worked throughout the Delta. He learned his trade well and when he, and Robert Jr. Lockwood, began appearing on a daily KFFA radio show in 1941 he was already a 'star' of the Delta blues scene. His performances on the fifteen-minute radio show *King Biscuit Flour Time* were, just like all his performances, a mixture of the musician, the raconteur and the showman all

"Just before we do this next number, ladies and gentlemen, tonight's a big night in Greenwood, Mississippi, yes, sir. Meet me there, beat me there." ~ *Sonny Boy promoting his own gig on the* King Biscuit Flour Time *radio show*

thrown together in a seductive blues package. Sonny Boy used the radio to promote his evening performances, which got club owners to pay him better money as more people visited their club; it also helped in advancing Sonny Boy's career as the show was networked to WROX-radio in Clarksdale, Mississippi and KXJK-radio, Forrest City, Arkansas.

He worked on *Sonny Boy's Cornmeal and King Biscuit Show* until 1948, and his face was printed on the bags of cornmeal to sell the product. Sonny Boy and Robert Lockwood began calling themselves the King Biscuit Entertainers and evolved into a full-blown band that included, at various times, pianists Dudlow Taylor, Pinetop Perkins and Willie Love, with Peck Curtis on drums and Houston Stackhouse on guitar.

The *King Biscuit* show was one of the most popular on the radio, even spawning its own blues song, 'The King Biscuit Stomp,' recorded by Big Joe

KING BISCUIT TIME
RADIO STATION
K.F.F.A.

KING BISCUIT
49 LBS
KING BISCUIT
THE KING OF FLOURS
FANCY PASTRY & BISCUIT
FLOUR
Guaranteed by
BUHLER MILL & ELEVATOR CO.
BUHLER, KANSAS

KING BISCUIT
TIME
Radio Station
K.F.F.A.
Helena, Ark.

GLADIN'S STUDIO
HELENA, ARKANSAS

"He was, in fact, one of the most genuinely creative, persuasive, strikingly individualistic performers the blues has ever seen." ~ *Pete Welding's sleeve notes for the Chess album* One Way Out

Williams in 1947. Among those that Sonny Boy also appeared with were Howlin' Wolf, on the *Hadacol Show* on KWEM that broadcast from West Memphis, and Elmore James, on the *Talaho Syrup Show* on WAZF that broadcast from Yazoo City in Mississippi. Hadacol was a patented vitamin supplement that was popular throughout the South, probably because it contained 12 percent alcohol.

Sonny Boy was one of the biggest names around Memphis and the Delta in those days as B.B. King attests. "I got to audition for Sonny Boy, it was one of the Ivory Joe Hunter songs called 'Blues of Sunrise.' Sonny Boy had been working out of a little place called the 16th Street Grill down in West Memphis. So he asked the lady that he had been working for, her name was Miss Annie, 'I'm going to send him down in my place tonight.' My job was to play for the young people that didn't gamble. The 16th Street Grill had a gambling place in the back, if a guy came and brought his girlfriend or his wife that didn't gamble my job was to keep them happy by playing music for them to dance. They seemed to enjoy me playing, so Miss Annie said if you can get a job on the radio like Sonny Boy, I'll give you this job and I'll pay you twelve dollars and a half a night. And

I'll give you six days of work, room and board and man I couldn't believe it."

Despite being well known in black households across the South his recording debut was not until 5 January 1951, for Lillian McMurry's Trumpet label at their studio at 309 Farish Street in Jackson, Mississippi. It featured pianist Willie Love, Elmore James, Joe Willie Wilkins, and drummer 'Frock' O'Dell. None of these sides were released at the time. His first recording to be released was made on 12 March 1951. It was the classic 'Eyesight To The Blind' which featured Willie Love on piano, Henry Reed on bass and Joe Dison on drums; this song would later feature on The Who's 1969 *Tommy* album.

More Trumpet sessions followed between 1951 and 1954. Among the other sides he cut for the label were 'Nine Below Zero' and he played harmonica on Elmore James's classic 'Dust My Broom.'

While Sonny Boy would later re-record many of his early, self composed, recordings these early sides capture the feel of his raw juke-joint blues to perfection.

Such was his skill with the harmonica that he could put the entire harp in his mouth and still draw the notes. Whenever he played his harp he

Left to right: Willie Nix, Sonny Boy Williamson and Robert Jr. Lockwood

"Sonny Boy Williamson, a completely captivating singer and harmonica master whose mysterious, wizard-like appearance belies the fires beneath."
~ Max Jones, Melody Maker, *28 September 1963*

THINKS...
I'll NIP DOWN THE OL
CRAWDDIDY
RICHMOND ON FRIDAY AND HEAR
LESTER SQ. AND THE G.Ts
THEN OVER CROYDON ON SAT.
FOR A BIT OF THE
AUTHENTICS
AND A QUICK PINT, THEN
BACK TO RICHMOND 4 SUNDAYS
YARDBIRDS!!
THEN I'LL HAVE TO CADGE
5/- OFF MUM SO'S I CAN
GO BACK DOWN CROYDON
ON WEDNESDAY AN' HEAR
SONNY BOY
THE OLD DEVIL!!
WITH THE
MULE SKINNERS
THEN ILL THINK ABOUT
PLAYING DADDY CRAWMUS!
H.

became the center of attraction, no matter how many and how good were the other musicians that were playing with him. He had a great sense of musical timing coupled with intricately woven phrases and a superb use of vibrato.

By 1955 Sonny Boy's contract had been sold on to Chess. He had for some time been playing in the bars of Detroit, where he worked with Baby Boy Warren, as well as in Chicago. His first sides for Checker, recorded in Chicago, feature Muddy Waters, Otis Spann, Jimmy Rogers and Fred Below. 'Don't Start Me Talkin'' was a great debut for the label, and eventually made No.3 on the *Billboard* R&B chart in fall 1955. Subsequent Checker sides saw him

reunited with Robert Jr. Lockwood, a happy state of affairs as Robert's playing perfectly complemented Sonny Boy's rhythmic sense. Living and working in Chicago did not stop him from returning periodically to Arkansas and taking up residency for spells back on the *King Biscuit Flour Time*. His traveling ways continued in 1963 when he was included in the second American Folk Blues Festival tour of Europe.

Sonny Boy loved Europe and Europe loved him, he even talked about taking up permanent residence, but initially he stayed behind in Britain after the tour ended. He recorded in Denmark with Matt 'Guitar' Murphy in November and then he recorded with both The Yardbirds and The Animals, playing club dates with both bands throughout Britain. Eighteen-year-old Eric Clapton was in The Yardbirds at the time

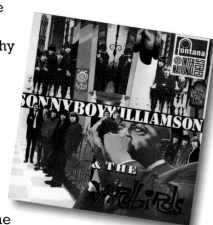

they recorded a live album at the Crawdaddy Club on 8 December 1963. The Yardbirds, with their teenage prodigy Clapton and the hard-drinking, hard-living Sonny Boy, must have been an impressive combination in the hot, sweaty clubs. Sonny Boy traveled throughout Europe and even played in Poland before appearing in the American Folk Blues Festival again in 1963 along with Howlin' Wolf, once again delighting audiences with his funny stories, casual asides and all-round showmanship. Shortly before he returned to America he recorded with organist Brian Auger and guitarist Jimmy Page.

By 1965, Sonny Boy had returned to Helena, Mississippi and yet another spell playing on the *King Biscuit* radio show. While Sonny Boy talked of returning to Europe it was not to be, and he died in his sleep in May 1965.

Sonny Boy's gravestone near Tutwiler, Mississsippi

"Sonny Boy was a bad influence on my soul."
~ James Cotton

Overleaf: The old Whitman Chapel cemetery on New Africa Road near Tutwiler, Mississsippi, the site of Sonny Boy's grave

Sonny Boy Williamson

BORN 4 December 1899 in Glendora, MS

DIED 25 May 1965 in Helena, MS

INSTRUMENT Harmonica, Guitar, Drums

FIRST RECORDED 1951

INFLUENCES John Lee 'Sonny Boy' Williamson

INFLUENCED James Cotton, Mojo Buford, Junior Wells, Muddy Waters, Howlin' Wolf

CLASSIC TRACKS 'Nine Below Zero,' 'Eyesight To The Blind,' 'Bring It On Home,' 'Don't Start Me Talkin''

HEARING THE BLUES

One Way Out   Chess

His Best   Chess

King Biscuit Time   Arhoolie

Blind Willie McTell

"No one can sing the blues like Blind Willie McTell." ~ *Bob Dylan*

DYLAN'S RIGHT, Willie McTell had a unique way of singing the blues; in his hands the blues were beautiful. But Blind Willie was not just a blues singer: he, like many of his contemporaries, sang a variety of material; he did rags, spirituals, and traditional songs nearly as often as he sang the blues. What sets Willie apart from many of his contemporaries is his sensitive vocal delivery. In many ways he is the total antithesis of what people think of as a country blues singer. He's the kind of blues singer to be played to someone who says they do not like the blues… they soon will.

No one is quite sure if William Samuel McTier was totally blind at birth, partially sighted, or became blind when he was a child or, perhaps, during his teens. Born in May 1901 in Thomson, Georgia, a small town about 100 miles to the east of Atlanta, his family moved to Statesboro from where he ran away from home to follow medicine and minstrel shows in his early teens. He's known to have been involved with the John Roberts Plantation Show; he was also, by this time, totally blind. Having learned the guitar from his mother when he was young he gave it up for about eight years, starting again while at the State Blind School in Macon sometime around 1922; according to his own testimony in 1940 he also went to a blind school in New York, and another Michigan, where he said he learned Braille. It was after this that he became a hobo, traveling around the East Coast, playing in parks and on street corners for loose change.

Willie McTell played a 12-string guitar, partly because he liked the sound, but also it was the ideal instrument for playing on the street. Louder than the 6-string, it allowed him to both attract an audience and then entertain the people as they grew into a large group of listeners. McTell was typical of his generation of blues singers; he sang a variety of material, performing rags, spirituals, and traditional songs nearly as often as he sang the blues. Given his vocal style some might think that Blind Willie was more of a folk singer than a blues singer, but even a casual listen will tell you he's singing the blues; it's just the different way he sings them. With his deft guitar playing and exceptionally warm voice some have likened him to a white man trying to sound black, which makes him immensely easy to listen to.

Long before he made any records, Willie McTell was a well-known figure on the Atlanta blues scene, he was a good friend of Curley Weaver and Buddy Moss. He was a regular at house rent parties, on street corners, at fish fries, and anywhere he could

"And the blues came down, like dark night showers of rain." ~ *Blind Willie McTell*

"You may search the ocean, you might go 'cross the deep blue sea. But Mama, you'll never find another hot shot like me."
~ Blind Willie McTell

get some money for performing his songs. Above all else these itinerant entertainers had to entertain; an audience would only put their hands in their pockets for a little loose change if they liked what McTell, and others like him, performed. He sometimes worked with others and in 1933 he is known to have played on street corners with Blind Willie Johnson, making a formidable pair of artists. It would have been truly amazing to witness these two great musicians working side by side. Both were masters of their craft, both blind, and they were brilliant guitar players that have inspired future generations.

Willie McTell made his living from playing for money wherever and whenever he could and the fact that he made records, just like for most of his contemporaries, was a little bonus and little else. It was on 18 October 1927 that the man who was called 'The Dean of The Atlanta Blues School' recorded for the first time. He cut four sides for Victor Records in Atlanta, then almost a year later to the day he recorded some more sides for Victor. At this second session he recorded his classic, 'Stateboro' Blues,' with three other sides, including 'Three Woman Blues.' Another year passed before he recorded again, this time as Blind Sammie for Columbia; it was the first of the pseudonyms he used to get around contractual liabilities. More sessions followed for Victor, and then he went back

into the studio for Columbia as Blind Sammie in 1930 and again the following year. At the session in October 1931 in Atlanta he recorded two of his best songs, 'Broke Down Engine Blues' and 'Southern Can Is Mine.'

By 1934 McTell had married Kate, who can be heard singing with him on some of his later records. He continued to record up until 1936 for Victor, Vocalion and Decca, working with Piano Red and Curley Weaver. Throughout this period he could be found playing for tips on Atlanta's Decatur Street, as well as hoboing through the South and East. In a nine-year career Blind Willie McTell recorded some 60 sides for Victor, Columbia, Okeh, Vocalion and Decca under a variety of pseudonyms, that included Blind Sammie, Georgia Bill, Hot Shot Willie and plain Blind Willie.

On 4 November 1940, Alan Lomax and his wife were driving through Atlanta when they spotted a

"Blind Willie McTell, he used to come by my house a lot, sit on the porch and play."
~ Piano Red

"I began to hear Blind Willie McTell. My blues-playing really came from Blind Willie McTell; it came from that alternating thumb-picking style, even when I played slide it sounded much more like Blind Willie than somebody from the Delta." ~ *Guy Davis, bluesman*

and 'Amazing Grace' was very redolent of his old playing partner Blind Willie Johnson. These were some of the best recordings that he ever made.

In the late 1950s and early 1960s many white singers began to rediscover Blind Willie's pre-war recordings and he influenced many, among them Bob Dylan. In 1993 Bob Dylan covered 'Broke Down Engine' on his *World Gone Wrong* album. The song mixes the metaphors of love and travel: trains were a common theme in the blues and Willie McTell made liberal use of the evocative railroad names. The 'B and O Blues' was named for the Baltimore and Ohio line; elsewhere he sings of the Southern Pacific. It extends the train metaphors that were regularly used in gospel songs that were coded references to slaves making a bid for freedom

Dylan was just one among many from the rock era who were influenced by McTell. Both the Allman Brothers and Taj Mahal were among a long list of artists that recorded 'Statesboro Blues,' a song written and recorded by Willie in 1929... it did both their careers a great service. Taj Mahal covered the song on his 1968 debut solo album. It was one of the

guitarist at the Pig 'n' Whistle rib shack, they stopped and found it was McTell. The next day they recorded him at their hotel room for the Library of Congress's Archive of American Folk Song. McTell played songs, including the blues and rags as well as talking about his life and other musicians, including Blind Willie Johnson. McTell's playing of spirituals including 'I Got to Cross the River Jordan'

"The blues for me is basically ancestor worship in the sense of accessing the great things that ancestors have done."
~ *Taj Mahal, 1999*

songs that reached a large number of people in Britain as a result of being included on the low-price CBS sampler album *The Rock Machine Turns You On*; it inadvertently introduced many people to

the music of Blind Willie McTell… and it did Taj Mahal's career no harm either.

In 1949 and 1950 Willie recorded again, mostly spirituals and other religious material, but his style was not what people wanted to hear by this time so he went back to singing on Atlanta street corners. He recorded once more in 1956 when an Atlanta record store manager, Edward Rhodes, discovered him playing on the street for quarters; he enticed him into his store with a bottle of corn liquor and captured a few final performances on a tape recorder that were released posthumously.

Blind Willie McTell died of a brain hemorrhage in August 1959. During his career he was not a big seller, but he has come to be regarded in later years as a great performer, someone to whom many acknowledge a debt.

Blind Willie McTell

BORN 5 May 1901 in Thomson (McDuffie Co.), GA

DIED 19 August 1959

INSTRUMENT Guitar, Harmonica

FIRST RECORDED 1927

INFLUENCES Blind Willie Johnson

INFLUENCED The Allman Brothers, Bob Dylan

CLASSIC TRACKS 'Statesboro Blues,' 'Three Woman Blues,' 'Broke Down Engine Blues,' 'Southern Can Is Mine'

HEARING THE BLUES

Blind Willie McTell 1940
Alan Lomax Recording

The Classic Years 1927-1940
JSP Records

The Definitive Blind Willie McTell *Sony*

King of The Georgia Blues
Complete Blues

Son House

"He was by far the most intense. If the blues was an ocean distilled to a lake, to a pond, to a pool, to a tub, to a glass and ultimately to a drop, the essence, the very concentrate, this is Son House." ~ *Dick Waterman*

THE MAN BORN Eddie James House Jr. in Riverton, deep in the Mississippi Delta, managed to have two careers as a blues singer, one short one back in the 1930s and another during the folk blues revival of the1960s. His pre-war career consisted of a few recorded sides made during a trip to Grafton, Wisconsin, the home of Paramount Records, which only sold in their hundreds. He like many of his contemporaries played the blues at local parties, fish fries and in juke-joints, rarely earning much more than the price of a few drinks. Yet this is a man that Muddy Waters referred to as a king.

Known as 'Son' House, his father played in the family brass band and he grew up on a plantation near Clarksdale. He was preaching in church by the time he was fifteen, as well as working a variety of jobs. He taught himself to play the guitar sometime around 1923 and was soon playing house rent parties and local picnics. Sometime in 1928 House shot and killed a man, it is said in self-defense, so he spent time at Parchman Farm; he was released in 1929 after a judge re-examined his case. After serving time he began playing levee camps and country dances around Clarksdale with Charley Patton.

Sometime around the middle of May 1930, House accompanied Patton north to Paramount's Grafton recording studio. With them on the trip were Willie Brown and Louise Johnson. With Willie Brown accompanying him, Son House recorded ten songs on Wednesday 28 May; subsequently eight were issued on four 78-rpm discs, for which he was paid $40. The one word that describes House's singing style is 'intense'; few blues singers, either before or since, have matched his intensity. When Son sang the blues you had to believe him. Apparently his sermons were as intense as his blues. Son's second record was the two-part 'Preachin' The Blues' in which he tells of how the blues stole him away from the church.

Oh I went to my room, I bowed down to pray
Oh I went to my room, I bowed down to pray
Sayin' the blues come along and they blowed my
spirit away

Oh, I'd have had religion, Lord this very day
Oh, have had religion, Lord this very day
But the womens and whiskey, well, they would not
let me pray

"But the best we had to my ideas was Sonny House. He used to have the neck of a bottle over his little finger, touch the strings with that and make them sing. That's where I got the idea from." ~ *Muddy Waters*

House was one of the creators of the Delta blues sound, his emotional intensity coupled with his forthright guitar style influenced many that followed, including Robert Johnson and Muddy Waters. His religious background combined with his secular music created what has been described as the forerunner of soul music.

Like many of his contemporaries Son fell victim of the Depression, and of the failure of Paramount. He simply went back to the Delta and carried on where he left off, playing the usual round of picnics, parties and poorly paid gigs. Their records hardly sold at all, like many other bluesmen who recorded just a few sides and then vanished. At 75 cents a record it was a lot for a poor black person to spend in those tough economic times. They possibly sold a few copies in the cities but with the cotton business suffering worse than many others the chances of them selling copies to people in the Delta were next to zero.

House's next recordings were in 1941 and were done with Alan Lomax for the Library of Congress, not designed to sell commercially but to become an important part of America's folk heritage. He recorded six songs at Lake Cormorant, Mississippi during the same few days as Lomax recorded Muddy Waters at Stovall's Plantation. Lomax again recorded House in 1942; soon after House moved to Rochester, New York where he worked for the railroad and later still as a barbecue chef.

He was not heard of again musically until 1964, when he was rediscovered in a poor state of health, with a drink problem, living in an apartment with his wife of 30 years. He was found by Dick Waterman, who tells how it came to pass during the summer of 'Mississippi burning.' "I promoted a week of shows with John Hurt in

"And with him the sorrow of the blues was not tentative, or retiring, or ironic. Son's whole body wept, as with his eyes closed, the tendons in his powerful neck standing out with the violence of his feeling." ~ *Alan Lomax*

February 1964 and then I did another show with Bukka White. He said that he had seen Son House alive in Memphis (this eventually proved to be a false trail). I gathered up two guys and went down to Mississippi in the summer of 1964. Looking back over it - three Jewish kids had a yellow Volkswagen with New York plates; we had no sane reason to be here, but we were looking for Robert Johnson, Son House, Skip James, any of them we could find. We ascertained that Johnson was dead and no-one had ever heard of Skip James or anyone who played like him, but we backtracked Son House. We found an old man whose son had once been married to Son's stepdaughter. Mrs House had children by her first marriage. So we found him and he said 'Yes, I was once married to the daughter of Son and Mrs House.' Then we found her, 'Oh, yes, they came over to Detroit a couple of years ago.' We got someone on the phone, Son didn't have a phone at that point, and he brought a man to the phone – Sunday 21 June 1964. So we said, 'Are you the Son House that recorded with the Library of Congress and recorded for Lomax? Did you know Charley Patton? Did you know Robert Johnson? Did you use to live in Robinsonville?' And there was this long pause, and he said, 'Who is this anyway? Yes, that's me, I done all those things.' And we said, 'OK, don't go anywhere. We're on our way.' And he was in Rochester, New York. So we had gone from Cambridge, Massachusetts, down to the Delta and turned around and went back up to Rochester, New York."

Shortly after finding House, Waterman introduced him to Al Wilson, who later joined Canned Heat. House was due to play the Newport Folk Festival and as Wilson played his bottle neck guitar in open-neck tuning he was the ideal one to relearn House his songs… because he hadn't played them for 16 years or more. Waterman later recalled that Al Wilson literally taught Son House how to play Son House. His performance at the Festival set House on the road to a broader audience appeal than he could ever have imagined when he was recording in the 1930s.

In June 1965 Dick Waterman took Son to meet Muddy Waters at a gig. They had not seen each other for over 20 years. One of Muddy's band started poking fun at House and in an instant Muddy was standing over the guy, grabbing him by the throat. 'Don't you be mocking that man.' And everybody just went 'Wow.' And Muddy said, 'Don't you be making fun of him. When I was a boy coming up, that man was king, you hear me? That man was king. Here you are mocking and making fun of him. If it wasn't for that man you wouldn't be here because you wouldn't have a job because I wouldn't

One Night Only! · Friday Night July 22
The Roundhouse
Chalk Farm Road London NW1 8EH
Located 100 yards from Chalk Farm Tube, opposite the ESSO garage.

Admission £4   Reservations 020 7424 6772

In Person! LIVE
The Great SON HOUSE

★ James Cotton
★ Buka White
★ Lousiana Slim
★ Willie "Big Eyes" Smith
★ Bob Margolin
and
★ Birdlegs & Pauline
will join together on the main marquee stage!

Other surprise guest stars!!

BLUES

"My dad was a student of Son House. He learnt a lot of stuff from him, watching him. Son House was a powerful, powerful performer."
~ *Big Bill Morganfield, (Muddy Waters' son)*

be here. Don't you ever make fun of that man; he was king when I was a boy coming up.'

He signed to record for CBS, and his album *Father of The Folk Blues* gave him the opportunity to play in America and Europe. After spending the first few years of the 70s touring he again retired, to live in Detroit. He lived another 14 years and died aged 86.

Son House

BORN 21 March 1902 in Riverton (Coahama Co.), MS

DIED 19 October 1988 in Detroit, MI

INSTRUMENT Guitar, Dobro

FIRST RECORDED 1930

INFLUENCES Charley Patton, Willie Brown

INFLUENCED Robert Johnson, Muddy Waters, Howlin' Wolf, Sonny Boy Williamson

CLASSIC TRACKS 'My Black Mama,' 'Preachin' The Blues,' 'Dry Spell Blues,' 'John the Revelator'

HEARING THE BLUES

Father of the Delta Blues –
The Complete 1965 Sessions
Sony

Son House Revisited
Varese Sarabande

Delta Blues   Snapper

Tampa Red

"One of the blues' most fluent, inventive and hence influential guitarists and... one of its foremost, perennially fertile original song writers." ~ *Pete Welding,* Down Beat, *1975*

THE MAN WHO GOT his nickname from the town of his youth and the color of his hair, cut his first record for Paramount in 1928. Later he switched to Vocalion and then in 1934 to Victor Records, recording hundreds of sides before America declared war on Japan; they sold in vast numbers, making him one of the biggest stars of the 1930s. Yet today he's rarely a name that's mentioned by people recalling the pre-war blues greats. Dubbed the 'Guitar Wizard,' Tampa's slide-playing and single-string picking on a National steel-bodied resonator guitar were influential to many that came to follow him.

Tampa Red's real name was Hudson Woodbridge, although he later went by the name Hudson Whittaker after his parents, who were probably not married, split up and he lived with his maternal grandmother. He came from Florida and moved to Chicago in his early twenties, playing on the streets and in dives; he was 24 years old when he cut his first side for the Paramount label sometime in May 1928. By September he switched to Vocalion, where his debut 'It's Tight Like That,'

sold in large numbers and established his reputation. Accompanying him on piano was Georgia Tom Dorsey; together they invented the 'hokum style' of blues. Hokum, with its light, almost jazzy, melodies along with humourous and sometimes risqué lyrics, became all the rage. So popular was their debut, and the sound of hokum, that they were often billed as The Hokum Boys or Tampa Red's Hokum Jug Band, which sometimes included Frankie Jaxon on vocals as well as a variety of other musicians. Frankie 'Half Pint' Jaxon was unusual for a blues performer; he was a female impersonator

Tampa's style was the very antithesis of Delta blues; he sang directly to the newly arrived city-dwelling blacks by creating a sound of urban sophistication that also attracted aspiring city dwellers still stuck in the country. His partnership with Dorsey ended in 1932, soon after they cut the excellent 'You Can't Get The Stuff No More.' Georgia Tom, disillusioned with the blues, turned to God, and gospel music; in all they cut close to 75 sides together, including 'The Ducks Yas Yas Yas' (one of

"Tampa Red, he was a good ol' guy."
~ *Arthur 'Big Boy' Crudup*

"Tampa Red's house was a madhouse for old-time musicians... Tampa Red's wife would be cooking chicken and we'd be having a ball."
~ Willie Dixon

the few examples of rhyming slang in the blues).

Tampa signed to the Victor label in 1934 and stayed with them for 20 years. Victor's subsidiary, Bluebird, pitched him to different markets, sometimes billing him as Tampa Red and the Chicago Five, with records in a dance band style. On others he was simply Tampa Red, although he was usually accompanied by a pianist (often Black Bob) or Willie B. James on second guitar; these were more straightforward blues songs. Historians have argued that Bluebird was attempting to have Tampa 'cross over' to the white market; superficial evidence supports this. Some of his releases had white artists on the flip sides of the records, notably Bill Boyd's Cowboy Ramblers in 1936. What is more likely is that the budget label, Bluebird, selling at 35 cents, was using Tampa as their 'race' entry into the dance band market. Tampa, along with his wife Frances, ran a Chicago boarding house for musicians, at 35th and State, which was fondly remembered by many including Big Bill Broonzy, Memphis Slim and Big Maceo.

Tampa, a prolific songwriter, worked with pianist, Big Maceo in 1942, although sales had started to drop off. By the late 40s Tampa was recording with

"They only have one fairly smutty meaning." *~ Tampa Red on rock'n'roll in 1960*

pianists Blind John Davis, Big Maceo and Johnnie Jones. In 1953 he cut four sides with Big Walter Horton on harmonica, but when his wife died the following year it hit him hard and he declined thereafter, with alcohol taking its toll.

His last recordings in 1960 included the wonderfully titled 'Don't Tampa With The Blues,' an album on Bluesville Records. It is a poignant recording, which featured reworkings of his biggest hits, along with some other classic blues tunes; it was just Tampa, his guitar and kazoo. The man whose early career was built on the double entendre, recording classics like 'Let Me Play With Your Poodle,' was somewhat disparaging about rock'n'roll in 1960 around the time of the album's release, which is somewhat hypocritical, but it does prove that even musicians get more conservative as they get old.

Ironically Tampa may have had more to do with rock'n'roll than he or anyone else thinks. In 1929, Tampa Red's Hokum Jug Band recorded, 'My Daddy Rocks Me (With One Steady Roll),' which is the earliest example of the words 'rock' and 'roll' appearing in a song title.

My man rocks me with one steady roll
It makes no difference if he's hot or cold
When I looked at the clock, clock struck one.
I said honey oh let's have some fun
But you rock me with one steady roll

Something sound a little familiar? Shades of Chuck Berry? Was it coincidence, divine inspiration or a great memory? When Chuck's recorded 'Reelin' and Rockin' in 1957 he sang, "Well I looked at my watch it was 9.21. Was at a rock'n'roll dance, having nothing but fun." Proving the old adage that there's no such thing as new ideas, just old ideas thought of again.

T-Bone Walker

"T-Bone used to use a lot of horns. They made a beautiful sound, like shouting in the sanctified churches, in just the right places. He had a good rhythm section too. And to me T-Bone seemed to lay right in between there somewhere. It was the best sound I ever heard." ~ *B.B. King*

IF YOU ASK ANY OF THE GREAT GUITARISTS that came along in the 1950s and 60s who influenced them then probably every one of them will say T-Bone Walker. He almost single-handedly created the modern electric guitar blues sound that has been championed by everyone from B.B. King through to Otis Rush, Eric Clapton, Stevie Ray Vaughan and Jimi Hendrix. Not only was he a brilliant guitarist whose 'shuffle' rhythm was such a trademark but he was the quintessential showman.

Aaron Thibeaux Walker's grandmother was a Cherokee Indian and both his parents were musicians; he was born in rural Texas and his family moved to Dallas when he was two years old. He sang in church and when he was in his late teens he was often to be found leading Blind Lemon Jefferson along Central Avenue in Dallas so he could play for tips. Self-taught Walker began by playing guitar at local parties sometime around 1923, later touring in medicine shows where he also worked with the female blues singer Ida Cox. He made his first recordings in 1929 as Oak Cliff T-Bone for the Columbia label; while 'Trinity River Blues' and 'Wichita Falls Blues' have Walker playing guitar, the dominant instrument is Douglas Finnell's barrelhouse piano. What's abundantly clear from these two sides is T-Bone's distinctive voice.

Some short time after his recording debut, Walker went to Oklahoma City where he learned to single-pick notes on his guitar from a man named Chuck Richardson. Along with him was his boyhood friend, Charlie Christian, who, in the late 1930s, became one of the top jazz guitarists and an inspiration within jazz circles, like Walker in the blues.

"When I got older, maybe 12, I could play the ukulele, and I entertained at church picnics or at Riverside Park." ~ *T-Bone Walker*

"He was a figure of major importance... playing the kind of lean, biting guitar licks and solos which turned a generation of blues and R&B exponents around in new directions."

~ *Max Jones,* Melody Maker

In the early 1930s, T-Bone played all over Texas as a member of various bands, but in 1934 he moved to California where he frequently worked the Little Harlem Club as well as other Los Angeles venues. By the late 1930s, Walker had begun to experiment with the electric guitar; it was arguably one of the great experiments in modern music. It led to him joining The Les Hite Orchestra to record 'T-Bone Blues' in June 1940. Two years later he signed to Capitol Records and began working as the featured guitarist with the Freddie Slack Orchestra, as well as recording in his own right. Slack, an excellent boogie-woogie pianist and veteran of Jimmy Dorsey's band, was

white, and his band was of mixed race. Slack soon found success, and helped establish his fledgling new record label, Capitol, when 'Cow Cow Boogie,' featuring the excellent Ella Mae Morse, made the charts in late 1942. Two of the sides T-Bone cut with Freddie, 'I Got A Break, Baby' and 'Mean Old World,' did much to establish T-Bone's standing with those that followed. Both sides were seminal in creating what we now refer to as the West Coast blues sound; mellow and polished riffs, the epitome of laid back. While the sound was neither as definitive nor as successful as the Chicago sound it has an important place in the story of the blues, as well as rock and pop music, especially in the immediate post-war period when the 'West Coast Sound' did much to prepare the ground for rock'n'roll.

It was during this period that Walker developed his stage act, which included doing the splits while playing the guitar behind his head and playing it between his legs; this was later copied by Jimi Hendrix and Chuck Berry to great effect. But it was not all flash; there was a huge amount of substance

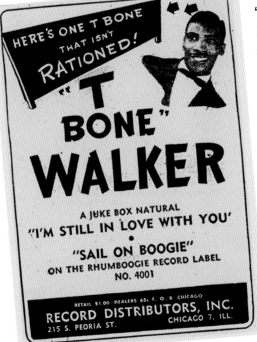

"Everybody listens to T-Bone."
~ *Otis Rush*

"While we're doing that blues thing, we're going to play you a T-Bone Walker song."
~ Duane Allman at the Fillmore East, acknowledging their debt to the great man

to the way he played. His intricate jazz chords, coupled with his superb tone and sense of dynamics, made Walker an inspiration. He had a sense of 'oneness' with the guitar that few since have been able to match.

By 1946 Walker was back in California, having spent a lot of time in New York and Chicago. In Los Angeles he signed to the Black and White label and in 1947 he had his first R&B hit when 'Bobby Sox Blues' (it's about Frank Sinatra) got to No. 3 in the chart. Over the next two years Walker had seven more R&B hits including 'T-Bone Shuffle.' One of those hits was 'Call It Stormy Monday (But Tuesday Is Just as Bad),' which he recorded in mid-1947 in Hollywood and released just before Christmas. In early 1948 it climbed to No. 5 in the R&B charts. It's one of those records that has had a far greater impact on an artist's career, as well as music in general, than its original chart position would perhaps have you believe. Its importance was acknowledged in 1991 when it was given a Grammy Hall of Fame award. T-Bone's version, with his laconic vocals, great brass arrangement and his deft touch (alternating between delicacy and attack) on the electric guitar has made this the definitive version. T-Bone, who would record the song a number of times during his career, was not the first to record it. Earl Hines had charted with the song in 1942, with Billy Eckstine handling the vocals. Other fine versions include Bobby Bland's 1962 chart hit, Muddy Waters, and The Allman Brothers from their *Live At the Fillmore East* album in

1972. A few months after recording 'Stormy Monday' T-Bone cut 'T-Bone Shuffle,' which has become an essential piece for every aspiring blues guitarist to learn.

In 1950 Walker joined the Imperial label where he went on to record 52 sides, which are a remarkably consistent body of work. They demonstrate the wonderful rapport between his voice and guitar; they are the very embodiment of post-war sophisticated blues. While none could match his earlier chart success, he continued to be an inspiration for every guitar wannabe, and those that did be.

A switch to Atlantic in 1955 was to produce the last of his great recordings, most notably the 1959 album *T-Bone Blues*. During his time with Atlantic he recorded with Junior Wells and modern jazz guitarist Barney Kessel. Towards the end of the 50s his alcohol

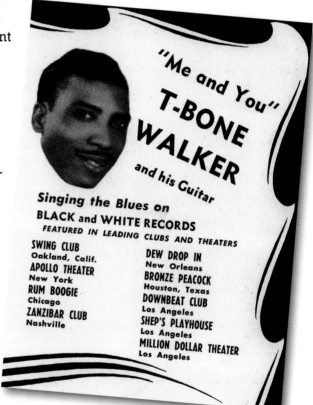

"Me and You" T-BONE WALKER and his Guitar

Singing the Blues on
BLACK and WHITE RECORDS
FEATURED IN LEADING CLUBS AND THEATERS

SWING CLUB
Oakland, Calif.
APOLLO THEATER
New York
RUM BOOGIE
Chicago
ZANZIBAR CLUB
Nashville

DEW DROP IN
New Orleans
BRONZE PEACOCK
Houston, Texas
DOWNBEAT CLUB
Los Angeles
SHEP'S PLAYHOUSE
Los Angeles
MILLION DOLLAR THEATER
Los Angeles

> ## "I believe it all comes originally from T-Bone Walker. B.B. King and I were talking about that not long ago and he thinks so too."
> ~ *Freddie King, 1971*

problems and a recurring ulcer increasingly began to affect his life. In 1962 Walker appeared in Europe for the first time as part of the American Folk Blues Festivals, and returned a number of times during the decade. His performances became less frequent in the U.S.A. as the 60s progressed, and he recorded sporadically. In 1970 he won a Grammy with the album *Good Feelin'*, but his stomach ulcer was getting no better and he could not give up the drink. In 1972 he was back in Europe with the American Folk Blues Festival.

In 1974 he suffered a stroke, and by spring the following year the man who was called 'the bluesman with a jazz soul' was dead from bronchial pneumonia. Practically every guitarist owes a debt to T-Bone Walker; a casual dip into his

Cleveland's Finest Night Club Presents

T-BONE WALKER
Outstanding Guitar Stylist
OPENING MON., OCT. 10

DELLA REESE
Beautiful Recording Vocalist Now
Nightly Thru Sunday, Oct. 9

Ralph Wilson's Orch. Nightly

COMING ATTRACTIONS—HELEN MERRILL ON OCT. 17. ALSO, AT LATER DATES, AL HIB-BLER, ARTHUR PRYSOCK, THE DRIFTERS AND OTHER GREAT ACTS

the chatterbox

FREE PARKING LOT FOR PATRONS
5121-23 Woodland Avenue   John Ballard, Proprietor

T-Bone Walker

BORN   28 May 1910 in Linden (Cass Co.), TX

DIED   16 March 1975 in Los Angeles, CA

INSTRUMENT   Guitar, Organ, Piano

FIRST RECORDED   1929

INFLUENCES   Leroy Carr, Lonnie Johnson, Blind Lemon Jefferson

INFLUENCED   B.B. King, Buddy Guy, Eric Clapton, Otis Rush, Chuck Berry, Jimi Hendrix… everyone!

CLASSIC TRACKS   'T-Bone Blues,' 'Call It Stormy Monday (But Tuesday Is Just As Bad),' 'Strollin' With Bone,' 'Vida Lee'

HEARING THE BLUES

T-Bone Blues   *Atlantic*

The Complete Imperial Recordings   *EMI*

T-Bone Blues: The Essential Recordings   *Essential*

The Complete Capitol & Black and White Recordings   *Capitol*

Howlin' Wolf

"He wasn't just a blues singer, I mean he was a commander of your soul, and he got hold of you with the blues. The Wolf was a hypnotizer, he hypnotized himself when he opened that mouth and let it loose." ~ *Sam Phillips, 2000*

THE BOY WHO WAS BORN Chester Burnett in the heart of the Mississippi Delta in 1910 grew up to be a powerfully built giant of a man; he also became a giant of the electric blues who has influenced just about everyone who played rock in the later half of the 20th century. The Rolling Stones covered one of his finest songs and took it to No.1 in the UK charts – something unheard of for a blues record. Many modern-day rock stars have idolized him, while others have looked to match the intensity of his performances – few succeeded in matching this most electrifying blues giant.

To begin with he lived around Aberdeen, Mississippi, singing at a Baptist church before his family moved to the Young & Myers Plantation, in Ruleville, Mississippi in 1923. The boy became Howlin' Wolf, acquiring his nickname because he was not the best-behaved child. At over six feet tall and weighing in at over 250 pounds he was an imposing figure of a man, who as a youngster learned to play the guitar from watching Charley Patton; he also picked up some of his onstage antics. It was Sonny Boy Williamson (Rice Miller) who taught him to play the harmonica; an impeccable musical pedigree. Above all else it was Wolf's singing rather than his playing skills that commanded an audience's attention – particularly when he played live.

Like many before him, Wolf started out playing wherever he could, local parties, clubs or just on the street. He served in the army during the war, moving to West Memphis at the end of the 1940s to spend a little more time performing, rather than farming. He put a band together that included both Little Junior Parker and James Cotton, got a regular gig on KWEM, a West Memphis radio

"I remember when he used to play out on the streets – he started down here in Ruleville, Mississippi, playin' on the streets and blowin' his harp." ~ *Muddy Waters*

his recording break in 1951 through Ike Turner, who was an unofficial scout for Sam Phillips' Sun label based at his Memphis Recording Studios at 706 Union Avenue. Phillips had set up his studio in January 1950 to record "anything, anytime, anywhere." Sam would take his equipment in his car to record weddings, parties or business meetings. At the same time he began to record local artists, and sell the recordings to established labels like 4 Star Records, Modern Records and their subsidiary RPM. In 1951 Sam also established a relationship with Chess Records. Among the blues artists he recorded were Lost John Hunter and Joe Hill Louis.

station, and performed and promoted his own live shows.

When he first recorded at Sun Studios, the Wolf was already over 40 years old; up until then he had spent his life farming and performing, not necessarily in equal measure. Perhaps that is why he was such a powerful performer, in the purest Delta tradition. He more than most post-war bluesmen conveys the feeling of Delta dirt. He got

Sam Phillips' masterstroke was not to overproduce but to allow his performers to cut through on record; it was a triumph of spontaneity over technical expertise. Sam's first hit was Jackie Brenston's 'Rocket 88' which was recorded in

"Well, Howlin' Wolf was one of the most interesting people that I worked with. He had probably the most God-awful voice you ever heard. It was so distinctive, so pronounced, that whatever you heard come out of his mouth, it had that magic charm of 'I believe this, I just believe it.' The Wolf would get in there and go into a trance." ~ *Sam Phillips*

Another Smash Hit on Chess . . .

"OH RED"

by

THE HOWLING

WOLF

Chess No. 1528

CHESS 750 E. 49th Street
Chicago 15, Illinois
RECORD CORP.

would remain his instrumental foil for the rest of his career. Wolf, along with Muddy Waters, cut the most influential set of recordings of any post-war Chicago bluesman; both men were also highly competitive with each other.

By the 1960s Wolf's chart career was over, but his powerful influence, through his recordings and his live work, continued to be felt. Albums like *Moanin' At Midnight*, *Howlin' Wolf* and *The Real Folk Blues* were keenly studied by younger musicians, especially the white blues players, both for new material and Wolf's technique.

Horst Lippmann and Fritz Rau, German blues lovers and promoters, created the American Folk Blues Festival in 1962, taking T-Bone Walker, Memphis Slim, Sonny Terry & Brownie McGhee, John Lee Hooker, Shakey Jake, and Willie Dixon to Germany to play a few dates. The following year the tour was also taken to Britain for the first time and among those appearing were Muddy Waters, Memphis Slim, Sonny Boy Williamson, Otis Spann, and Lonnie Johnson. In 1964, Sonny Boy was back along with Sleepy John

Memphis and leased to Chess Records in Chicago. Having been brought in by Turner, Wolf cut 'Moanin' At Midnight' and 'How Many More Years' which became his first single when Phillips sold the sides to Chess (R&B Chart No. 4). Wolf was soon also recording for Modern as well, and after some contractual wrangles he ended up with Chess, which is why, soon after, he moved to Chicago where he began the most prolific, and successful, part of his recording career.

Among his recordings were 'Smokestack Lightning,' 'Spoonful,' 'Saddle My Pony' (Charley Patton's song), 'Little Red Rooster,' 'Evil,' 'Back Door Man,' and 'Killing Floor.' After his debut he only charted three more songs during the 1950s, of which 'Smokestack Lightning' was the most successful. In Chicago, Wolf began an association with the brilliant Hubert Sumlin, the guitarist who

Coming To Cleveland For First Time, Opening Mon., Nov. 14

Howling Wolf!

And His Great Blues Band, Stars Of "Sure Nuff Blues"

Now Nitely Thru Sunday, Nov. 13

MUDDY WATERS

AND HIS GREAT ORCHESTRA

Bringing To Gleason's Some Of The World's Best Blues, Rock and Rhythm

MUDDY WATERS

MAMBO MATINEE 5 TO 8 EVERY SUNDAY

GLEASON'S MUSICAL BAR
5219 WOODLAND

"I was at these shows in shabby, provincial England in the mid-60s." ~ *Robert Plant*

Estes, Howlin' Wolf, Hubert Sumlin, and Lightnin' Hopkins among the performers; Wolf's appearance inspired many who were there.

Six weeks before Wolf appeared on stage in England at the Fairfield Halls, the Rolling Stones went into Regent Sound Studios in London to record Wolf's 'Little Red Rooster.' If you play their version right after Howlin' Wolf's original it's like a mirror. Wolf howls, Mick purrs, but it's what the blues are all about. Sex. The Stones' single came out a month after the American Folk Blues Festival show in London and went to No. 1. For some reason the Stones' label in America wouldn't release it as a single. But in May 1965 they got some kind of revenge when they were invited to play the *Shindig* TV Show in Hollywood. On the show were Jackie de Shannon, Adam Wade, Sonny & Cher and, at the insistence of the Stones, Howlin' Wolf. Today it is difficult to comprehend the enormity of seeing Wolf on what was very much a 'television show aimed at white kids, this was just two years after Martin Luther King's 'I had a dream speech.'

Expatriate Englishman Jack Good, who constantly referred to Wolf in his very proper accent as 'Mr. Howling,' produced *Shindig*. Wolf sang 'Smokestack Lightnin'' and while he was rehearsing for the show, Son House and his manager Dick Waterman came by the studio. "We talked our way in. I knew Wolf because he had played in the Boston area. Wolf saw Son and recognized him; it was like an elephant coming out of a phone booth. He came up in sections and Son looked at him and says, 'Man, he has got his growth,' because Wolf was

"I'm mainly a folk singer but I do some rhythm'n'blues songs." ~ *Howlin' Wolf, 1964*

"Howlin' Wolf's voice, dark, brooding, vibrantly rich and immediately recognizable, easily transcended the most banal material." ~

Amy O'Neal, Living Blues *magazine*

about 260 pounds. Brian Jones was watching me and then came up and tapped me and said, 'Excuse me, who is the old man that Wolf thinks is so special? Wolf is in awe of that old man, who is the old man?' And so I said, 'That's Son House.' And he turned to me and said, 'Ah, the one that taught Robert Johnson.'"

Wolf played the Newport Festival in 1966 and appeared at other festivals throughout the U.S.A. In 1970 he recorded *The London Howlin' Wolf Sessions* with Eric Clapton, Charlie Watts, Stevie Winwood, Ian Stewart and Bill Wyman. Wolf had already suffered a heart attack and there are signs of his failing health on the recording, but it still proved to be an inspiration for the younger white performers.

A car accident in 1971 caused irreparable damage to his kidneys, and an inevitable slowdown in live work followed. He also continued to record, although his once-powerful voice was showing signs of wear. In July 1975 the Rolling Stones were playing in Chicago and Bill Wyman went to Wolf's house for dinner. After they had eaten,, Bill asked to hear some of Wolf's records but he just pointed to an empty wire

record rack and said, "I've got none. I've given them all away to people who come to the house asking for my records." The following night Bill arranged for Wolf and his wife to go to the Stones concert. According to Wolf's wife, Lillie Burnett, "You should have seen the Wolf. It was just wonderful. We went to the concert and Bill Wyman must have arranged something, because when the Wolf walked into the stadium a spotlight went on him, and the whole place stood up and cheered. It was so good for him."

Wolf's last performance was in Chicago during November 1975 with B.B. King. At the end of the year he was admitted to the Veterans Administration Hospital in Chicago where they operated on the 65-year-old bluesman, but he died of kidney failure on 10 January 1976.

Sam Phillips, Wolf's producer at Sun Records.

"It's unfortunate that I didn't get to record the Wolf a lot longer, because he would have been my entirely different approach to rock'n'roll."
~ Sam Phillips, June 2000

Howlin' Wolf

BORN 10 June 1910 in West Point, MS

DIED 10 January 1976 in Hines, IL

INSTRUMENT Guitar, Harmonica

FIRST RECORDED 1951

INFLUENCES Charley Patton, Tommy Johnson, Sonny Boy Williamson (Rice Miller), Jimmie Rodgers

INFLUENCED The Rolling Stones, Cream, The Yardbirds, Captain Beefheart

CLASSIC TRACKS 'Smokestack Lightning,' 'Little Red Rooster,' 'Spoonful,' 'Killing Floor'

HEARING THE BLUES

Howlin' Wolf   Chess

Moanin' at Midnight   Chess

The London Howlin' Wolf
Sessions   Chess

The Definitive Howlin' Wolf
Geffen

Robert Johnson

"The root source for a whole generation of blues and rock'n'roll musicians."

"The most emotionally committed of all blues singers."

"The greatest singer, the greatest writer."

"The greatest folk blues guitar player that ever lived."

"The most accomplished and certainly the most influential of all bluesmen."

"He is a visionary artist."

THAT IS HOW ROBERT JOHNSON has been described by just a few of the musicians, historians and reviewers to have become fascinated by his life, his playing and his music since he was rediscovered in the late 1950s and early 1960s. It's little wonder that the man's life and work have become the stuff of legend with so much mystery surrounding his personal life; a life that lies juxtaposed with his small, but incredible, body of recordings. Robert Johnson has been an inspiration to probably more musicians than any other single blues artist, or almost any musician for that matter, of the 20th century.

Details of Robert Johnson's life are, to say the least, sketchy, and despite recent research that has helped shed more light on his short life, the very fact that the facts are hard to glean have in their own way contributed to his legend. These then are the things that we are fairly certain about.

Johnson's mother, Julia, had ten children before Robert was born, all ten being born in wedlock; her husband's name was Charles Dodds. Julia was probably around 40 years old when Robert was born illegitimately; his father was a plantation worker called Noah Johnson. Charles Dodds had moved to Memphis as a result of problems he was

"I kind of got hooked on it because it was so much more powerful than anything else I had heard or was listening to. Amongst all of his peers I felt he was the one that was talking from his soul without really compromising for anybody." ~ *Eric Clapton*

having with some prominent Hazelhurst landowners. Robert was sent to live with him when he was around three or four years old, by which time all of Charles's children had moved to Memphis.

Growing up in Memphis, he first learned the basics of the guitar from his brother. Then, aged around eight or nine, Robert moved back to the Delta to live with his mother and her new husband Dusty Willis; for a while he was known as Little Robert Dusty. By all accounts Robert was more interested in music than he was in working in the fields, which put him at odds with his stepfather. In 1930, by the time he was 19, Robert had married a girl of 16 but she died shortly afterwards while giving birth to their child.

It was around 1930 that Son House moved to live in Robinsville, which is when young Robert would have first heard him play. House recalled many years later that "he blew a harmonica and he was pretty good with that, but he wanted to play guitar." It was from House and Willie Brown that Robert learned. He would watch them play and when they took a break he would use one of their guitars; according to House he was not good at all,

"...such a racket you never heard!... get that guitar away from that boy," people would say, "...he's running people crazy with it." By 1931 Robert had married again but at the same time he had started to travel, all the while improving his guitar skills through playing juke joints and picnics throughout the Delta and possibly farther afield. A year or so later, Robert returned home and played for Son House and Willie Brown who were staggered by his improvement. "He was so good. When he finished, all our mouths were standing open."

Johnson again resumed his itinerant ways, his reputation growing as he played. By this time he was traveling further afield, visiting Chicago, New York, Detroit and St. Louis that we know of for sure.

All this playing was important as it helped to develop his 'audience technique'; it also seems to have fueled his reputation as a womaniser. His 'technique' seems to have centered on concentrating his performance on just one woman in the audience; there's little doubt that this approach helped in securing one-night stands, as well as relationships that lasted longer, with a number of different women. Johnson traveled and played with Johnny Shines, who later recalled that

"He was in a little town called Frye's Point, and he was playing on the corner there. People were crowdin' round him, and I stopped and peeked over. I got back into the car and left, because he was a dangerous man... and he really was using the git-tar, man..." ~ *Muddy Waters*

Robert was always neat and tidy, despite days spent traveling dusty Delta highways. Johnny also recalled that Robert was just as likely to perform other people's songs as he was his own. He did everyone from Bing Crosby to Blind Willie McTell and Jimmie Rodgers to Lonnie Johnson. Robert, like many others, performed the songs that earned him money, songs his audiences requested. Like many of the itinerant bluesmen, playing songs for a few cents turned them into a human jukebox

By the time Robert Johnson was in his mid-twenties he took a trip to H.C. Speir's store in Jackson, Mississippi. Like many of his contemporaries he wanted to make some records. Speir was a part-time record scout for the ARC label, so by late November 1936, Johnson had travelled to San Antonio to record the first of his twenty-nine sides. On Monday 23 November he cut 'Kind Hearted Woman Blues,' the first of thirteen takes of eight different songs. Three days later he was back and cut '32-20 Blues' and then the following day he cut nine more takes on seven different songs. He then took a train back to

Mississippi and his life as an itinerant musician, although he was temporarily richer having pocketed money from his recording session; it is doubtful whether it was more than $100.

The first of Robert Johnson's records to be released was 'Terraplane Blues' coupled with 'Kind Hearted Woman Blues'; it would be the only one that sold in any great number at the time. His next release, '32-20 Blues' along with 'Last Fair Deal Gone Down,' was followed by 'I Believe I'll Dust My Broom' and 'Dead Shrimp Blues.' Sales were not fantastic but clearly good enough for him to be summoned back for more recording. This time he went to Dallas and recorded three more sides on 19 June 1937. The following day he cut thirteen more takes of ten more songs.

After his second recording session, Johnson went 'touring' in Texas, along with Johnny Shines. They played jukes, parties and dances, as they did in the Delta, before heading back to Mississippi via Arkansas. Precise details of the last year of his life are somewhat imprecise, although it is known that Robert spent some time in Memphis and

"Sometimes he'd be the most mild-mannered, quiet person you'd ever meet. At other times he would get so violent so suddenly, and you couldn't do nothing with him." ~ *Johnny Shines*

Helena, Arkansas. Gayle Dean Wardlow, a Mississippi journalist, went in search of Robert Johnson's death certificate, finding it in 1968; it confirmed that Robert had died in Greenwood on 16 August 1938 aged 27 years old.

One of the key myths that has dogged Robert Johnson concerns his death... was it murder? While we know when he died we only have hearsay evidence as to precisely how it happened. It is believed that he was playing a juke attached to the Three Forks store near Greenwood, Mississippi. According to David 'Honeyboy' Edwards he was poisoned at the store. He got so sick that he had to be taken the three miles into Greenwood where he died. The supposition is that Robert was having some sort of an affair with the

wife of the owner of the Three Forks, and it was he that poisoned Robert. Through the research of Gayle Dean Wardlow it has come to light that on the back of the death certificate was information that points to the fact that Johnson may have been born with congenital syphilis. According to a doctor it is possible that he had an aneurysm caused by the syphilis and his penchant for drinking moonshine.

Having died in mysterious circumstances it seems only right that Johnson's place of burial should be equally shrouded in ambiguity. We have visited three places at which he may have been buried. One has a headstone erected by Sony Music, at another location, a headstone paid for by the members of ZZ Top. Yet another has no headstone and is just one of those graveyards that 'could' be the place. In 2000, an 85-year-old lady named Rosie Eskridge said that her husband helped to bury Johnson in a graveyard about three

"Keith Richards is still very much a bluesman. His god is still Robert Johnson." ~ *Mick Jagger*

Above: Little Zion Missionary Baptist Church, Greenwood, where Rosie Eskridge claims her husband helped bury the body of Robert Johnson.
Right: The gravestone donated by Sony Music at Mount Zion churchyard, near Morgan City, Mississippi

"These men, supposed to be illiterate, Robert Johnson – a fine poet." ~ *Taj Mahal*

The gravestone at Payne Chapel, near Greenwood, paid for by ZZ Top.

asking, they just go to the junction of Highway 61 and Highway 49 and have their photograph taken. Sad to say the current crossroads of the two highways is at least half a mile from the one that would have existed in Johnson's lifetime. The point is, there is no actual crossroads.

In 'Cross Road Blues' Robert is singing of man's need to make choices – the fundamental choice between good and evil. In the Delta the story goes that if a bluesman waited by the side of a deserted country crossroads in the dark of a moonless night, then Satan himself would come and tune his guitar. A story made more relevant, in the construction of the Johnson myth, when coupled with Johnson's frequent references to the Devil. In his songs like 'Me And The Devil Blues,' in which he tells of "Me and the Devil was walkin' side by side," 'Preachin' Blues (Up Jumped The Devil)' and 'Hell Hound on My Trail,' aspects of Johnson's deal with the Devil help fuel the rumors

miles from Three Forks. Other people have talked of at least two other locations for Johnson's final resting place. Maybe it's just as well that no-one really knows.

Probably the most famous myth of all, the one that has inspired, fascinated and taxed everyone, is the one that tells of Robert Johnson selling his soul to the Devil. For decades people have gone to the Mississippi Delta, stopping people in the street or asking in shops or bars where they will find Robert Johnson's crossroads. Delta residents are apt to roll their eyes, some will even send unsuspecting blues tourists off deep into the backcountry to where they will swear they will find THE crossroads. Other visitors do not bother

While the myths surrounding Robert Johnson

"His supreme sense of time, which permitted him to break tempos and to sing over implied rather than stated rhythms." ~ *Alexis Korner*

"I would like to have written that." ~ *Bono of U2*
talking about 'Hell Hound on My Trail'

are numerous, there's no doubting the fact that he has influenced just abut every blues musician that has followed him as well as numerous rock guitarists who are in awe of his ability to play complex patterns and rhythms. But Robert Johnson was also influenced by a dozens of different musicians and their recordings. Tracing the roots of his songs has become a fascinating study for blues lovers and historians alike. Some are songs that Johnson would have heard on a record, the radio or he might have heard his contemporaries playing live, just like he did, to earn a few dollars.

Everyone in the 1930s came under the influence of Leroy Carr. In 1935 at their final session he and Scrapper Blackwell recorded 'When the Sun Goes Down.' Two years later Johnson used Leroy's song as the inspiration for the melody and feel of 'Love in Vain'; Johnson was also influenced by Carr on 'Kind Hearted Woman Blues.' It was not just black performers that Johnson must have listened to because 'Phonograph Blues' is clearly influenced by white country blues player Cliff Carlisle's 'That Nasty Swing.' Skip James, another of the great Delta bluesmen, can clearly be heard to have inspired Johnson on '32-20 Blues' (James had '22-20 Blues') and 'From Four Until Late' (James' 'Four O'clock Blues') and 'Hell Hound on My Trail' has its roots in

Skip's 'Devil Got My Woman.'

Others that influenced Johnson's recorded songs were Kokomo Arnold, The Mississippi Sheiks, Hambone Willie Newbern and Lonnie Johnson. The story of 'I Believe I'll Dust My Broom' is the most complex of all and it is featured on the biography of Elmore James elsewhere in this book.

Whatever their influences, Johnson's records have attracted collectors ever since interest in him began to take hold in the latter part of the 1950s and in 1961 when CBS released *The King of the Delta* LP. It sent eager collectors off in search of their own piece of Delta blues and specifically the original Vocalion 78-rpm shellac recordings on their blue labels. For a man who got around $200 for his work in the studio, Johnson would be staggered at the value of his records in the 21st century. An ARC release of 'Cross Road Blues' coupled with 'Rambling on My Mind' is worth in excess of $12,000. The least valuable of an original 78-rpm record is still worth around $3,500. If you see one, buy it, they will only go up in value. When *The King of The Delta Blues* was re-released in 1998 on CD it contained a newly discovered alternate version of 'Traveling Riverside Blues' as a bonus track

Every year it seems that some new aspect of Robert Johnson is there to be discussed, dissected or even exploited. In 1986, as if the legend needed

it, there was a movie called *Crossroads*, directed by Walter Hill and starring Ralph Macchio and Joe Seneca, with music by Ry Cooder. The story is not specifically about Robert Johnson, more a mix of his life and the fantasy legend of Faust. In 1994 the U.S. Post Office decided to issue a stamp commemorating Robert Johnson; they did so having airbrushed out the cigarette that he was smoking. Every now and then, new photographs of Johnson turn up, or at least photos that are claimed to be genuine images of the the most elusive of all bluesmen. Several years ago some film footage that purported to show Johnson was offered for sale until it was proved to be nothing of the kind.

How long will the Robert Johnson myth be mulled over by musicians, historians and blues lovers? Just as long as people are fascinated by his music, which probably means forever.

"You might not hear another Robert Johnson or a Muddy Waters. That won't happen. For some reason that's a miracle time; it just came and it went."
~ *Ry Cooder*

The store at Three Forks, near Greenwood, Mississippi where Robert Johnson is reputed to be have been poisoned.

Overleaf: The old crossroads of Highway 61 and Highway 49 in Clarksdale, Mississippi.

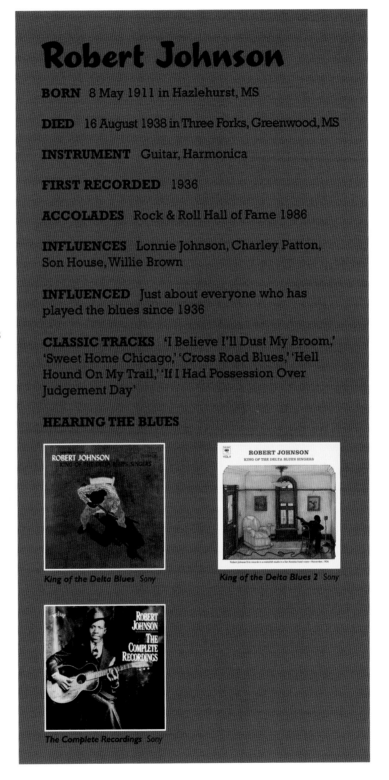

Robert Johnson

BORN 8 May 1911 in Hazlehurst, MS

DIED 16 August 1938 in Three Forks, Greenwood, MS

INSTRUMENT Guitar, Harmonica

FIRST RECORDED 1936

ACCOLADES Rock & Roll Hall of Fame 1986

INFLUENCES Lonnie Johnson, Charley Patton, Son House, Willie Brown

INFLUENCED Just about everyone who has played the blues since 1936

CLASSIC TRACKS 'I Believe I'll Dust My Broom,' 'Sweet Home Chicago,' 'Cross Road Blues,' 'Hell Hound On My Trail,' 'If I Had Possession Over Judgement Day'

HEARING THE BLUES

King of the Delta Blues Sony

King of the Delta Blues 2 Sony

The Complete Recordings Sony

Lightnin' Hopkins

"People have learned how to strum a guitar, but they don't have the soul. They don't feel it from the heart. It hurts me. I'm killin' myself to tell them how it is." ~ *Lightnin' Hopkins*

TEXAS BLUESMAN Lightnin' Hopkins was another whose career was both long and fruitful. He performed live for six decades and recorded for over 30 years, amassing a catalog that was larger than almost any of his contemporaries'. Not only was he prolific, but also he was also a great raconteur and a very good live performer with an 'act' honed to perfection at pre-war dances and parties. His guitar playing was unconventional, some have even called it ragged, but it is not as a guitarist that he will be remembered. Somehow the way he set his songs seemed totally apposite and it gave everything he did an authenticity that few others were able to match.

Born Sam Hopkins, his father was a musician who died when Sam was very young. The family moved to Leona in Texas where he grew up; in 1920 he watched Blind Lemon Jefferson at a picnic in

Buffalo, Texas, which inspired him to make a 'cigar box' guitar. His older brother Joel taught him to play the homemade guitar before his mother, Frances, encouraged him to play organ at her home church services. However, he was drawn to the music played by his older brothers, Joel and John Henry. He soon dropped out of school and like most people with his kind of background Sam worked on the plantation. "I did a little plowin' – not too much, chopped a li'l cotton, pulled a li'l corn. I did a little of it all." He, like many other bluesmen, began playing at picnics and dances at local farms on a Friday and Saturday night; later he took to hoboing throughout Texas.

At the end of the 1920s, he formed a partnership with his cousin, Texas Alexander, and the two of them played on street corners for tips. Their partnership continued until the mid 1930s when

"Well sometimes they wanted the blues played, but they most was really dancin' you see... it's different now. Everybody wants the blues. They don't want too many boogies."
~ *Lightnin' Hopkins talking to Paul Oliver*

"His blues are poetic, personal recollections and observations, and he delivers them with a sense of humor and sincerity."

~ Chris Albertson's album notes on Lightnin' Hopkins

Hopkins was sent to Houston County Prison Farm for some unknown offense. After his release, he rejoined Alexander working at picnics, parties and juke joints, as well as working outside of music. He would travel around Texas, often on buses, where the drivers would even let him ride for free as long as he played for the passengers.

In 1946, Hopkins and Alexander were offered a recording contract by an Aladdin Records talent scout. Inexplicably, only Hopkins followed up the offer when Lightnin' and his manager Lola Ann Cullum made the trip out West to Los Angeles to record on 4 November 1946. He cut 'Katie Mae Blues' with pianist Wilson 'Thunder' Smith; they were billed as Thunder and Lightnin'. It was a hit in the Southwest so Aladdin got him back into the studio a year later when he recorded 'Short Haired Women,' which sold around 40,000 copies. In 1948 he sold over twice that many records with his recording of 'Baby Please Don't Go,' almost all of them around the Houston area and his home state.

At the same time as recording for Aladdin (he would record 43 sides in all for the label), he cut records for Goldstar in Houston. Sometimes it was the same songs; in fact he would go on to make records for over twenty different labels during his long, drawn-out recording career. If he was not the most prolific blues recording artist, his discography was certainly the most complex to unravel. He made the R&B charts in 1949 with 'Tim Moore's Farm'; over the course of the next three years he had four more hits, the biggest being 'Shotgun Express,' which made No.5.

Hopkins had a five-year hiatus away from recording between 1954 and 1959, although he did make a couple of records in 1956. With the rise and rise of Chess Records, electric blues was what the fans wanted and to many, Hopkins seemed old fashioned. In 1959 he was 'rediscovered' by folklorist Mack McCormick and his career was revived when Sam Charters recorded him for the Folkways label. The following

"He is, in the finest sense of the word, a minstrel: a street-singing, improvizing songmaker born to the vast tradition of the blues. His music is as personal as a hushed conversation." ~ *Mack McCormick*

year, he played Carnegie Hall with Joan Baez and Pete Seeger as well as playing at the University of California Folk Festival, in Berkeley, California, and touring the college circuit. He got to an even wider audience when he appeared on the CBS TV special *A Pattern Of Words & Music*.

Throughout the 1960s his prolific output appeared on a variety of labels. His preferred method of recording was to get the money up front. To Hopkins, royalty payments were far too insecure a way of earning a living; Lightnin' did not like to waste a lot of time so he usually did only the one take. After his Carnegie Hall appearance, he began to play more prestigious venues, including, the Newport Folk Festival, as well as touring Europe with the American Folk Blues Festival in 1964. He sometimes appeared with Clifton Chenier's Band and in 1967 he featured in a film short made by Les Blank entitled *The Sun's Gonna Shine*. The following year Blank made another short, *The Blues According' To Lightnin' Hopkins*.

Like many of his contemporaries he too recorded something of a progressive electric blues album – *The Great Electric Show & Dance* – but it was not a setting in which Hopkins felt comfortable. During

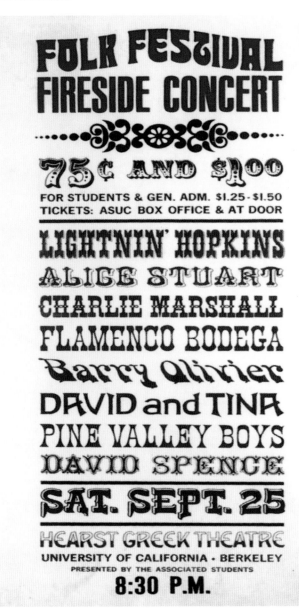

the 1970s he remained very active in the recording studio as well as playing live. He played throughout the U.S.A. and Canada and again crossed the Atlantic to appear in Britain, despite his dislike of flying. In 1970 he was featured in the British TV show *Blues Like Showers Of Rain* and the following year on PBS TV in *Artists In America* and *Boboquivari*. As the 80s rolled around he was beginning to see a downturn in the appeal of his unique brand of Texas country blues, and was also having some issues with his own health. He died of cancer in Houston, Texas in January 1982.

"He was not one that liked publicity. I remember talking to him one time at a blues singer's funeral. They were taking pictures, and the newspapers were around, and he'd say, 'Ah don' wan' none o' that at my funeral.'"
~ Bertha Kelly, Lightnin' Hopkins' granddaughter

Lightnin' Hopkins

BORN 15 March 1912 in Centerville, TX

DIED 30 Januray 1982 in Houston, TX

INSTRUMENT Guitar, Organ, Piano

FIRST RECORDED 1946

INFLUENCES Blind Lemon Jefferson, Texas Alexander, Lonnie Johnson,

INFLUENCED Lightnin' Slim, J.B. Lenoir

CLASSIC TRACKS 'Short Haired Woman,' 'Mojo Hand,' 'Penitentiary Blues'

HEARING THE BLUES

Lightnin' Hopkins
Smithsonian Folkways

Mojo Hand: the Anthology
Rhino

Lightnin' Hopkins Sings The Blues Crown Records

Country Blues
Essential Media GRP

Muddy Waters

"Muddy, he can really sing the blues. I mean the country, wide-open blues. He ain't like those pretty boy singers who dress up the blues so you don't know what it is... Muddy's a real singer of the blues." ~ *Big Bill Broonzy*

BANDLEADER, SONGWRITER, guitarist, singer, song interpreter and the prime mover of the Chicago electric blues scene, Muddy Waters (McKinley Morganfield) hailed from the Mississippi Delta, like almost all the great electric bluesman of the post-war era. He was also a good man who helped many younger or struggling musicians. But whatever else he was, he will forever be the once and future King of the Chicago Blues.

When he was about three years old, McKinley Morganfield's mother died, so he was sent to the Stovall farm to stay with his grandmother. After he grew up, he began working on the plantation, while at the same time teaching himself the harmonica and later the guitar. He began playing in juke joints, at parties and dances in and around the Clarksdale area from about 1935 onward.

In mid-summer 1941, Alan Lomax recorded Muddy at Stovall's for the Library of Congress; Muddy sang 'Country Blues' and 'Burr Clover Country Blues'. According to Howard Stovall, whose family still own the farm, "He was the burr clover man, which was a cover crop to put nitrogen back in the soil. It's drudge work, you hand rake it up and put it in bags and then spread the burrs around to improve next year's crop. I had the honor of that job one summer. Apparently Muddy felt about it the same way I did, only he was able to express it more eloquently."

In 1943, Muddy, who had got his nickname from his grandmother because he was always playing

"Muddy, one of the first guys to drive a tractor at our plantation, wasn't the most contented tractor driver in the world and he couldn't wait to get out of farming and into a life as an entertainer." ~ *Howard Stovall, 2000*

in a nearby creek as a child, moved north. He, like many before him, took the train to Chicago's Illinois Central Station, initially finding work in a paper factory. Muddy began playing for tips on Maxwell Street soon after arriving in the city, and Big Bill Broonzy helped the country boy break into the urban scene. He started working in clubs, playing with Eddie Boyd, as well as backing Sonny Boy Williamson No.1 at the Plantation Club. A switch from acoustic to electric guitar in 1944 galvanized Muddy's career. He continued to play traditional Delta bottleneck, but the electric guitar transformed his sound and helped to 'invent' post-war Chicago blues. His 1946 recordings for Columbia with the doyen of Chicago blues, Lester Melrose, went unreleased. It was not until the following year that Muddy would be heard playing on record, in the role of backing guitarist to Sunnyland Slim.

Waters and bass player Big Crawford recorded two other songs on the day he worked with Slim, but Leonard Chess was unimpressed and so they went unreleased. However, the following year Muddy and Crawford were back and cut 'I Can't Be Satisfied' and 'Feel Like Going Home,' which Leonard Chess released on the Checker label. The former was a reworking of 'I Be's Troubled,' a song Muddy recorded for Lomax in 1941 and often played live. 'Feel Like Going Home' was a reworking of Son House's 'Walking Blues.' Muddy had huge respect for House and this is another song Muddy must have sung many times before this recording. The record sold out in less than a day, going on to make No. 11 on the R&B charts in September 1948; years later Muddy recalled that he even had trouble buying a copy. Chess was anxious not to upset a winning formula, and despite the fact that Muddy had his own band, he continued to record Muddy as a duo, or with Leroy Foster on guitar.

By the late 1940s, his band included Leroy Foster on guitar or drums, Big Crawford on bass and Jimmy Rogers on guitar and harmonica, and not long afterwards Little Walter Jacobs was added as the featured harmonica player. Muddy was only in his early thirties but he became the patriarch of the Chicago blues scene. With the pick of the city's musicians in the 1950s, it was more a question of who didn't play in Muddy Waters band than who did. The Muddy Waters Blues Band was recording as an entity by 1951, the epitome of the hard-edged, driving electric blues band of Chicago, a cornerstone of what we call rock music today.

In 1951 'Louisiana Blues' became the second in his run of sixteen chart hits, which included classics like 'I'm Your Hoochie Coochie Man,' 'Just Make Love to Me,' 'Mannish Boy' and 'Forty Days

"He'd always been kind to his family, he never got to a place where he thought he was better. He was always a humble person."

~ Pastor Willie Morganfield, Muddy Waters' cousin

and Nights.' The man born in Rolling Fork, Mississippi also cut 'Rollin' and Tumblin',' 'Rollin' Stone' and 'They Call Me Muddy Waters,' in which he sings "I'm the most bluest man in this whole Chicago town"… few would disagree. Any and every one of these recordings captures the very essence of 1950s Chicago blues.

In 1959 Muddy released *Muddy Sings Big Bill*, a tribute album to his former mentor who had died a year earlier. Muddy considered Big Bill to be 'the Daddy of the Country Blues singers," so when he first moved to the city it must have been amazing for the younger man to find such a star taking an interest in him. It also shows the similarity in style between the two singers. On the album Muddy is accompanied by his band of the moment, James Cotton on harp, Pat Hare on guitar and the brilliant Otis Spann on piano. They perform 'Just a Dream,' a perfect testimony to both men, and while Muddy makes the song his own, Big Bill comes shining through.

'I Feel So Good' from the album exemplifies Muddy's approach, brilliant interpretation and vocal delivery that is underpinned by tight ensemble playing. Otis Spann on piano, James Cotton's harmonica and Pat Hare's guitar are nothing but perfect. The following year at the Newport Festival, Muddy performed the

"I knew Muddy well, and played with him in the 1970s. He was very dignified, a man that you would easily respect, just from the way he carried himself. He was funny, and he was always so charming and sweet; he always had plenty of time to listen to other people talking." ~ *Bill Wyman*

Muddy Waters shows pianist Otis Spann a lick or two.

"He was such a sweet man, people like that shouldn't ever have to die." ~ *Buddy Guy*

song, to a predominantly white audience, and it was captured for his album *Muddy Waters at Newport*, one of the great live albums and a favourite of many blues fans. As the band powers through the song, the crowd can be heard responding to their brilliance with spontaneous shouts. Not that this one song was any different from many that Muddy performed, he affected everything he did with style and class.

Throughout the 1950s and early 1960s Muddy's band was Chicago's premier recording outfit, a veritable academy of the blues. Among those who played with Muddy were guitarists Jimmy Rogers, Luther Tucker, and Earl Hooker; harmonica players Junior Wells, Big Walter Horton and James Cotton, Willie Dixon on bass; pianists Memphis Slim, Otis Spann, and Pinetop Perkins along with drummer Fred Below.

Another was Buddy Guy, who played on Muddy's wonderful 1964 album *Muddy Waters Folk Singer*. He was another musician who had a lot to thank Muddy for. "My mother had a stroke and I left Baton Rouge, Louisiana 25 September 1957. And I went to Chicago. I actually was looking for just a regular job to help my mom, but I ran into a bad situation. I couldn't get work, nobody would hire me. I played on the street first, one day this man grabbed me by the hand and walked me in this club. It was Otis playing, the guy told Otis to call me up and I played 'Things I Used To Do,' and someone called Muddy on the phone. I was pretty

hungry 'cos it was the third day without food. Muddy came in and just smacked me and said wait a minute, I heard about you, they done call me and got me out the bed. He said you hungry, I said you Muddy Waters, I'm not hungry, I'm full, I met you."

Muddy Waters Folk Singer was loathed by some, as were two other albums in the same vein, but it shows the depth of his talent, his understanding of the blues and his brilliance in playing them in whatever form he wanted. Muddy, like many of his contemporaries toured Britain in the 1960s as part of the American Folk Blues Festivals; his reception was better than when he had previously visited at the invitation of jazz trombonist Chris Barber in 1958. Many people in the jazz fraternity, who were the keepers of the blues flame in 50s Britain decided it was a travesty for Muddy to play with amplification. Somehow these blues zealots decided that the only pure blues was acoustic – thank goodness ideas changed. In May 1964 Otis Spann cut a single at Decca studios in London with producer Mike Vernon. On 'Pretty Girls Everywhere' and 'Stirs Me Up.' Otis was

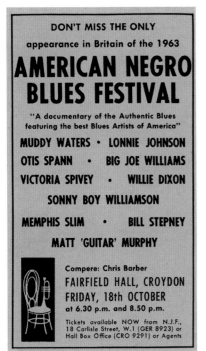

accompanied by Muddy Waters on rhythm guitar and Eric Clapton on lead. Some years later Eric recalled "they were both very friendly, and they had beautiful shiny silk suits with big trousers!"

As the blues languished somewhat in the late 60s, then so did Muddy's career. In the 1970s he toured constantly and by 1977 he had signed with CBS Records. Collaborating with Johnny Winter, Muddy's career took an upturn with the release of the album *Hard Again* in 1977, winning him a Grammy. A second album, *I'm Ready*, was followed by a tour of the U.S.A. including a performance at the White House for President Jimmy Carter.

Muddy worked live with Johnny Winter in the early 80s before succumbing to a heart attack in his sleep aged sixty-eight in 1983. Muddy's influence as well as the respect that he commanded among the rock community was acknowledged when he was inducted into the Rock & Roll Hall of Fame in 1987.

"No, I ain't no millionaire... but I had a lot of managers that became millionaires."
~ Muddy Waters

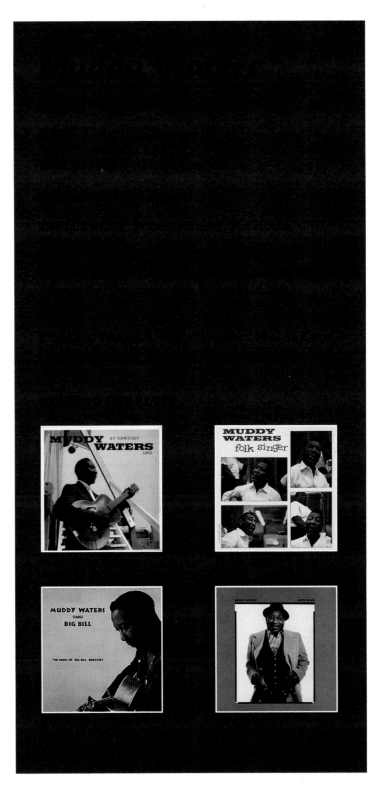

John Lee Hooker

"John Lee Hooker is a supreme force in American music. Listen to Jimi Hendrix's 'Blues Child,' listen to Van Morrison's phrasing, listen to nature's beat... it's keeping time with John's heart, foot and fingers. Boogie within, boogie without, but boogie till you shake off all your worries. John Lee is an ocean of inspiration." ~ *Carlos Santana*

FOR MANY PEOPLE who are under a certain age, John Lee Hooker was their personal invitation to enjoy the blues. He was of an age that made him accessible to many rock music fans that were anxious to explore the roots of the genre, especially his hard-edged electric guitar playing coupled with his forceful voice. He may also have been the busiest blues-recording artist of the postwar era, who later crossed musical paths with a whole host of modern-day guitarists and musicians in creating the now ubiquitous duet albums. While some have considered this a compromise, the four-times Grammy winner is a true original that brought people into the blues tent and what they found inside was never less than authentic.

John Lee was his mother Minnie's fourth child, who recalled his grandfather teaching him the rudiments of the guitar when he was a young boy. He grew up on the farm, where his stepfather, Will Moore, taught him the unusual foot-stomping guitar-playing technique that Hooker made his own. Like many of his contemporaries he first of all sang gospel music, but the blues soon took hold. Shortly before his fifteenth birthday, Hooker tried to join the army and spent three months in Detroit before they found out his real age; and sent him home to Mississippi, John Lee was firmly against a life spent working on the farm so he took to the road.

Hooker's first stop was Memphis, where he tried to establish his musical career while working as an usher in the Beale Street Theater. Whether the competition was too tough in the city that was the first stop north of the Delta, he was after all just a teenager, or there were simply too many blues players, no-one knows. Hooker left Memphis and went to Cincinnati where he worked in a variety of jobs; at night he played juke joints and house rent parties. He also returned to singing gospel music,

"My grandfather taught me to pick out harmony on strips of inner tube nailed in different tensions to the barn door."
~ John Lee Hooker

working with The Fairfield Four and The Big Six. In 1943 he went to Detroit where there was good-paying war work available and a burgeoning music scene on Hastings Street. Hooker became a big draw and was soon playing the Monte Carlo Club, Sporty Reed's Show Bar and the more upmarket Lee's Sensation.

Guitarist Eddie Burns: "He began to appear at the Monte Carlo and the Harlem Inn. When John Lee fell ill in 1950, I took over from him at the Harlem Inn. He was actually poisoned. Someone poisoned his whiskey and he almost died. I must say that he was a great womanizer, and it might have been a woman who wanted to kill him."

Hooker acquired a manager, Elmer Barbee, and in 1948 he engineered an introduction to Bernard Besman, the Ukrainian-born owner of Detroit's Sensation label. Besman decided to record Hooker, but interestingly he decided to lease his first two sides to Modern Records, a company with a far better distribution system. 'Sally Mae' was originally to be the A-side, but the B-side 'Boogie Chillen" quickly captured the record-buying public's imagination; it was a shrewd move in retrospect as 'Boogie Chillen" went to No. 1 on the R&B chart in January 1949.

Hooker, or The Boogie Man as he had been nicknamed, had three more top ten hits in 1949 as his career took off with 'Hobo Blues,' 'Hoogie Boogie' and 'Crawling King Snake.' Then in 1951 he again topped the chart with the classic 'I'm In The Mood,' co-written with Jules Taub. Hooker overdubbed his vocal three times, which helped to give the recording such a powerful resonance.

In early 2000, a CD featuring John Lee Hooker playing in a Detroit house in 1949 had its first release. Gene Deitch, a keen music fan, heard

"Every song I sing is something that happened to my life or somebody else's life. That's why everybody digs the blues… it has more feeling than other music. When I sing these songs I feel them down deep and reach you down deep." *~ John Lee Hooker*

Hooker play in a club and invited him for dinner and then recorded him singing and playing acoustic guitar. It is remarkable that the tape survived, and it demonstrates the influences that Hooker had already taken on board in developing his unique 'electric blues' sound. He performed 'Catfish Blues,' which Hooker was to cut many times in his career, as well as standards like 'Trouble in Mind,' 'How Long Blues' and 'In the Evenin' When The Sun Goes Down,' and spirituals like 'Moses Smoke The Water' and the folk standard 'John Henry' in which Hooker created his own melody.

Hooker recorded at a prodigious rate, and tracking his recordings is tricky as he, like many others, recorded under numerous pseudonyms for a variety of different labels; he was probably the busiest blues-recording artist of all during the early 1950s. Despite being under contract to a number of labels, he recorded for a variety of independent labels as Texas Slim, John Lee Cooker, Delta John, Birmingham Sam, Johnny Williams, The Boogie Man, John Lee Booker, John L. Hooker, John Lee Hooker, and even Little Pork Chops. "I cannot accurately recollect how many times I have cut records. I think that I've made discs for about thirty different labels," he admitted in the summer of 1964 while touring Britain with John Mayall's Bluesbreakers.

In 1962 Hooker visited Europe as part of the first American Folk Blues Festival. Seen by many of Britain's young musicians, he became a major influence for the aspiring blues players who would help create rock music. Around the time of his first trip to the U.K. he recorded 'Boom Boom,' another of his best-known tunes for Vee-Jay. He left the label in 1964, going on to record for a number of labels that included Chess and Verve-Folkways. 1964 was a time when the blues were making a big impact on the record buyers in Britain. Howlin' Wolf's 'Smokestack Lightning' entered the chart in early June. A week later John Lee Hooker's 'Dimples,' originally cut for Vee-Jay in 1956, charted and spent the rest of the summer in the lower reaches of the chart. It was a song originally recorded back in 1956 for the Vee-Jay label along with guitarist Eddie Taylor. The week after Hooker charted, he supported the Stones at a gig at Magdalen College, Oxford, which must have been a thrill for the band who did so much to introduce rock into the mainstream. Four

"His chanting voice, inventive guitar, and insistent foot-tapping make for a one-man orchestra which is hard to beat."

~ Blind Al Wilson, Canned Heat

"It is the most erotic thing I ever heard."

~ Bonnie Raitt on John Lee Hooker's guitar playing

days later, Hooker and John Mayall's Bluesbreakers played with the Stones at an all-nighter at London's Alexandra Palace. Hooker even got to appear on the TV show *Ready Steady Go!* In 1965 he recorded with The Groundhogs, a British blues band; unfortunately it was a poor choice.

Hooker's influence spread in unusual ways. The Zombies, with Colin Blunstone's angelic vocals, recorded a song called 'She's Not There,' which ostensibly has little to do with the blues. However,

as Rod Argent, the group's keyboard player and the song's writer revealed… "If you play John Lee Hooker's 'No One Told Me' from the *Big Soul of John Lee Hooker* album you'll hear him sing 'no one told me, it was just a feeling I had inside.' There's nothing in the melody or the chords that's the same, it was just that little phrase." A decade later Santana was to record 'She's Not There,' which provided an interesting link to Hooker.

By 1970 Hooker had teamed up with Canned Heat to record *Hooker 'n' Heat*, and it became his best-selling album in years. During the lean blues years of the 70s and early 80s, Hooker recorded and continued to tour, before making a cameo appearance in the 1980 *Blues Brothers* movie; but by this time his was a career built on past glories not new triumphs. That is, until 1989, when he recorded an album entitled *The*

Healer with guest musicians, including Bonnie Raitt, Keith Richards and Carlos Santana on the title track. The album is assessed as the biggest-selling blues album of all time. 1991's *Mr. Lucky* reached No. 3, making John Lee Hooker the oldest artist ever to climb as high on the U.K. album chart; it too featured guest artists, including Van Morrison, Ry Cooder and Albert Collins. In 1992 Levi Jeans used a re-recorded 'Boom Boom' for a TV commercial, and it subsequently made No. 16 in the U.K. singles chart.

In 1994 Hooker, following a hernia operation, decided to slow down. He spent the second half of the 1990s in semi-retirement, recording sporadically but spending much of his time at home in the San Francisco Bay area of California. In 1997 he opened a club in the city – named John Lee Hooker's Boom Boom Room.

The blues reaped rewards far greater than his contemporaries could have imagined. He told a *Newsweek* reporter in 1995 "I got chauffeurs. I got a long stretch black limousine. Bar in it. VCRs, telephone, everything. I got a suit for every day of the week." It was a long, long way from Clarksdale. In 2001, just before he was about to start a tour of Europe, Hooker fell ill and died shortly afterwards. He was 83 years old. On his very last recording, which he made with the Italian singer, Zucchero, Hooker sang the words, "I lay down with an angel." John Lee Hooker lifted many people's spirits with his unique approach to playing the blues.

"I know why the best blues artists come from Mississippi, because it's the worst state. You have the blues all right if you're down in Mississippi."
~ *John Lee Hooker, 1964*

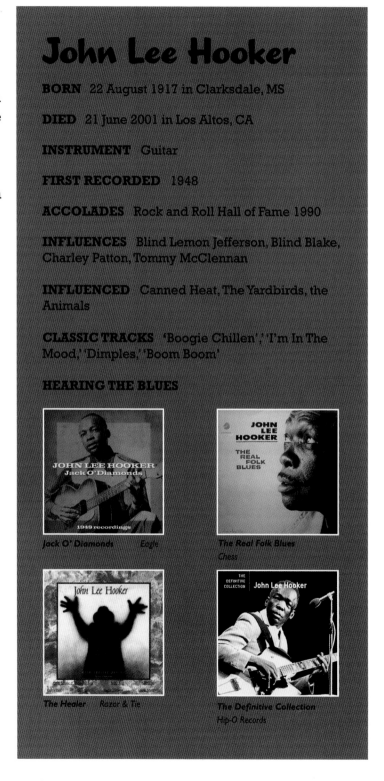

John Lee Hooker

BORN 22 August 1917 in Clarksdale, MS

DIED 21 June 2001 in Los Altos, CA

INSTRUMENT Guitar

FIRST RECORDED 1948

ACCOLADES Rock and Roll Hall of Fame 1990

INFLUENCES Blind Lemon Jefferson, Blind Blake, Charley Patton, Tommy McClennan

INFLUENCED Canned Heat, The Yardbirds, the Animals

CLASSIC TRACKS 'Boogie Chillen', 'I'm In The Mood,' 'Dimples,' 'Boom Boom'

HEARING THE BLUES

Jack O' Diamonds   Eagle

The Real Folk Blues
Chess

The Healer   Razor & Tie

The Definitive Collection
Hip-O Records

Elmore James

"His singing was as rough, violent and expressive as was his voice. Using the bottleneck technique most of the time, Elmore really let his guitar sound as I had never heard a guitar sound before. You just couldn't sit still! You had to move."

~ *George Adins watching Elmore James play in Chicago, 1959*

JAMES' PASSIONATE VOCALS and soaring slide guitar were one of the most effective trademarks of the blues. There is no doubt that he was one of the most important figures in post-war blues. He was the single most important slide guitar stylist of the post-World-War-II period and his playing had a huge impact on the sound of rock bands and their use of the electric guitar. Elmore James was the inspiration to legions of wannabe guitar heroes.

James was the illegitimate child of Leola Brooks, and was given the surname of his stepfather, Joe Willie James. His family moved around the Delta while he was a child, finding work picking cotton wherever they could. He taught himself the basics on a one-string homemade guitar, purchasing his first guitar in 1933, a $20 National. He started by playing house parties and juke-joints as Cleanhead and pretty soon he was playing gigs all over the Delta, making the acquaintance of other bluesmen including Arthur 'Big Boy' Crudup, Johnny Temple, and Luther Huff. By 1936, he had

moved to Belzoni, just off Highway 49.

In 1937, Elmore had moved to Greenville, Mississippi, where he met and played with Sonny Boy Williamson (Rice Miller) and Robert Junior Lockwood. It was here that he met Robert Johnson and probably first heard 'I Believe I'll Dust My Broom,' the song that was to establish James' reputation. There is speculation that it was Johnson that taught James how to use a piece of metal in order to 'slide' the notes on the guitar, a skill that James would come to master and introduce to many other guitarists. After working in a radio repair shop he served with the navy in the Pacific between 1943 and 1945. After the war he reunited with both Sonny Boy and his cousin, Homesick James, who both had radio shows on KFFA in Helena, Mississippi. Elmore was given some time on the shows, performing 'Dust My Broom,' among other titles.

Lillian McMurry, an independent record producer who owned Trumpet Records in Jackson, Mississippi, heard Elmore and wanted to record

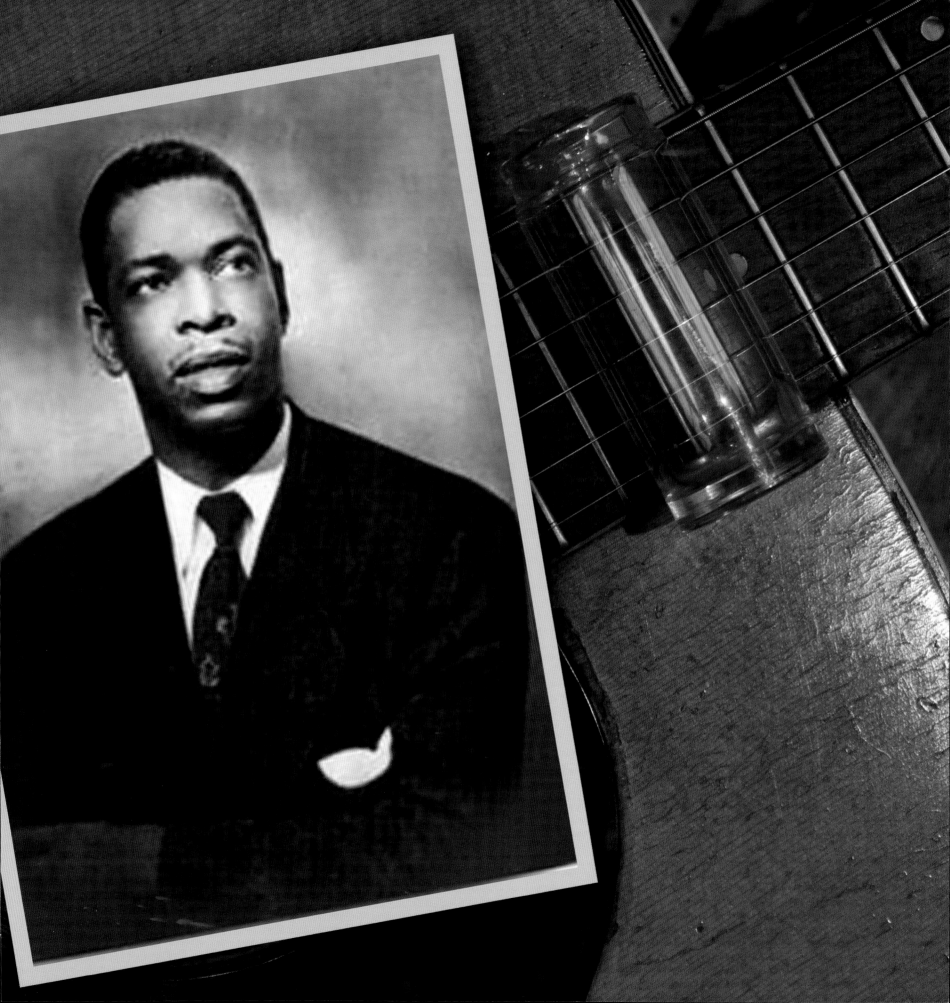

"Elmore James is an acquired taste, and I happen to really like Elmore James."
~ Frank Zappa

him, but he was painfully shy in the studio. They convinced him that he was rehearsing and did not tell him that they were recording 'Dust My Broom.' It was released on Trumpet 146 with Elmore, billed as Elmo James, on one side and Bo Bo Thomas singing 'Catfish Blues' on the other. The record made No. 9 in the R&B charts in April 1952.

Trying to recall where you first heard the quintessential electric blues riff that opens 'Dust My Broom' is difficult. It may have been the early 50s version by Elmore James or Fleetwood Mac's late 60s offering. Some may recall an unknown blues band at a club they visited in their youth; a few know it from the 1930s and Robert Johnson's supposed original. Or is Johnson's recording of 'Dust My Broom' the first version?

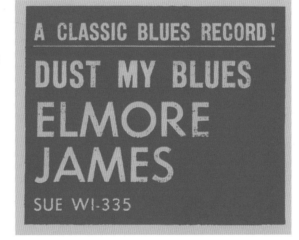

A CLASSIC BLUES RECORD!

DUST MY BLUES
ELMORE JAMES
SUE WI-335

In early December 1933, Roosevelt Sykes accompanied a singer named Carl Rafferty, a man about whom we know absolutely nothing, on 'Mr. Carl's Blues.' What we do know is this session was significant in the history of the blues. 'Mr. Carl's Blue's' contains the immortal lines, "I do believe, I do believe I'll dust my broom. And after I dust my

broom, anyone may have my room." Decades later, as historians dissected Robert Johnson's songs to understand his influences, it was generally assumed that the Delta blues legend based 'I Believe I'll Dust My Broom' on Kokomo Arnold's 'Sagefield Woman Blues.' Although the latter has words similar to 'Mr. Carl's Blues' it was recorded some ten months after Rafferty. We will never know who 'did it first,' but recorded evidence points to Mr Carl Rafferty accompanied by Mr. Roosevelt Sykes.

Several schools of thought exist as to the meaning of 'Dust My Broom.' It could concern cleaning a rented room before you leave – shades of the itinerant musician – or maybe it is simply a sexual reference. According to the singer Son Thomas, "it was an old field holler to tell everyone, except the people the hollerer didn't want to tell, that he was running away."

By early 1953 Elmore James had another top ten R&B hit, 'I Believe'; he had settled in Chicago and was working with a new backing band, The Broomdusters. In 1955 James re-recorded 'Dust My Broom' as 'Dust My Blues' with minor lyrics

"By then I was completely taken up with the blues and that led to Fleetwood Mac. All we were about was Elmore James." ~ Mick Fleetwood

schoolteacher rather than a blues guitar maestro.

In 1959 Bobby Robinson, the owner of Harlem-based Fire Records, searched for and found him, signing him to a contract. This gave Elmore a new impetus and he recorded some of his best music, 'The Sky Is Crying' made No. 15 in the R&B chart; it's one of his best numbers. If you want to know what makes the blues so powerful, then this song has imagery that stands up against the best lyrics of any musical form... "The sky is crying, look at the tears roll down the street." It's beautiful poetry. Elmore stayed with the Fire label until 1962, when problems with the musicians' union forced him to stop working union jobs.

It was around this time that Elmore's influence was being felt on the other side of the Atlantic in a way that would help to change the course of musical history. James was a major, maybe even the most significant, reason why the Rolling Stones came to be formed. In late 1961, Brian Jones went to see the Chris Barber Band in Cheltenham; the band featured Alexis Korner in a blues segment, which inspired the future Stone. After the show, Brian introduced himself to Alexis and while they chatted Korner told him about the gigs he played in London and encouraged Jones to visit. A month later Brian visited Alexis in London, which is when he heard his first Elmore James record; James went straight out and bought an electric guitar. Brian's early stage name was Elmo Lewis and his bottleneck guitar work paid tribute to James.

changes and a re-arrangement of the verses. It was credited to Johnson, arranged Elmore James & Bihari (Bihari is one of the two brothers who owned the Modern record label. James by this time was recording for Modern's subsidiaries, Flair and Meteor).

Elmore spent the rest of the 50s moving back and forth between Chicago and the Delta before he was diagnosed with a heart condition in 1957. Despite his health problems he continued to perform, but the lack of real recording success encouraged him get a job as a DJ in Mississippi, though he still kept making records, none of which were big sellers. His poor health made him thin and his heavy spectacles gave him the look of a

"I discovered Elmore James and the earth seemed to shudder on its axis." ~ *Brian Jones*

"King of the Slide Guitar." ~ *The words on his tombstone*

By 1963 Elmore James was once again recording, but on 24 May while he was at the home of Homesick James, in Chicago, preparing to go to the studio, he had a heart attack and died. He was 45 years old. In 1965 James had the last of his four R&B hits, almost two years after his death, 'It Hurts Me Too' made No. 25.

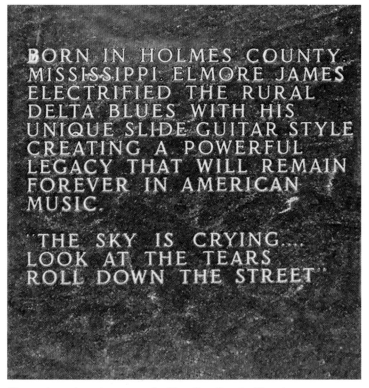

Elmore James' tombstone at the New Port Baptist Church cemetery, Holmes County, Mississippi.

Elmore James

BORN 27 January 1918 in Richland, MS

DIED 24 May 1963 in Chicago, IL

INSTRUMENT Guitar

FIRST RECORDED 1951

INFLUENCES Robert Johnson, Robert Nighthawk, Sonny Boy Williamson II, Charley Patton

INFLUENCED Homesick James, Johnny Winter, Brian Jones, Fleetwood Mac, Duanne Allman, B.B. King, J.B. Hutto

CLASSIC TRACKS 'Dust My Broom,' 'Shake Your Money Maker,' 'Done Somebody Wrong,' 'The Sky Is Crying'

HEARING THE BLUES

The Sky Is Crying   Rhino

Shake Your Money Maker
Buddha

Blues After Hours   Ace

*The Final Sessions – New York
1963*   Snapper

Jimmy Reed

"Down south, man, we always listened to the black stations – always – and we really identified with those guys because they were just doing it because it was fun. Even when Dylan came along, I'd still rather have listened to Jimmy Reed, and most of us felt that way." ~ *Stephen Stills, 1970*

JIMMY REED WAS ONE OF the most influential of the post-war bluesmen, yet his music is often ignored or forgotten today. His playing style was wonderfully rhythmic and his delivery of the blues was about as relaxed as you can get. He was also one of the most commercial bluesmen, who sold records in large numbers and had hits a-plenty on not only the R&B charts but also the *Billboard* Hot 100. In particular his influence on many of the early British beat boom bands was second to none; none more so than the Rolling Stones. Stylistically Reed was like no other and while his style may have gone out of fashion he deserves his place among the greats.

One of sharecroppers Joseph and Virginia Reed's ten children, he was born Mathis James Reed and lived on a plantation at Dunleith, near Leland, Mississippi. He learned to play guitar from boyhood pal and blues man Eddie Taylor, and sang with the Pilgrim Rest Baptist Choir from 1940 to 1943. He moved to Chicago in 1943 where shortly afterwards he was drafted into the U.S. Navy, serving until 1946. When the war was over he briefly went back to Mississippi before he and Taylor moved back to Chicago. By 1949 they were playing clubs, and sometimes Reed worked the streets for tips along with Willie Joe 'Jody' Duncan . With Taylor he played Velmas Tavern in Chicago, the Pulaski Hall in Gary with Albert King, and by 1952 he had a residency with the Kansas City Red

"It was honest and simple... and it drew its strength from the authenticity and clarity of Reed's observations about the everyday affairs of ordinary people." ~ *Pete Welding*

"We might not make this one." ~ *Jimmy Reed on one of his recordings sounding the worse for wear*

Band at the Black & Tan Club in Chicago Heights. Having initially cut some sides for the Chance label in 1953, Reed and Taylor tried out for Chess but they were rejected; maybe Chess thought they were a little too laid back when compared to what most of the artists on the label were like. Reed then signed to the newly formed Vee-Jay records; husband and wife Vivian Carter and Jimmy Bracken started the label out of their store, Vivian's Record Shop. By 1955 Reed began his impressive run of hits on America's rhythm & blues chart; his first was 'You Don't Have To Go,' by 1957 he had crossed over to the Hot 100 with 'Honest I Do' (No. 32). His other successes included 'Ain't That Lovin' You Baby,' 'You've Got Me Dizzy,' 'Bright Lights Big City' and 'I'm Gonna Get My Baby.' His four-beat walking-bass patterns made his records just perfect for the jukebox and for dancing.

Some commentators have given a large dollop of credit to his long-term guitarist and partner Eddie Taylor, who played on nearly all of Reed's sessions in the 1950s. There's also the strange case of Jimmy's wife, Mary Lee 'Mama' Reed, who helped write many of his songs as well as sitting behind him both in the studio and when they played live, whispering the lyrics in Reed's ear.

She's audible on several recordings, including 'Big Boss Man,' and there's no doubt she played a crucial role. Yet it was still Reed that sang them and his role should not be downplayed too significantly.

From 1958 to 1963, always accompanied by Eddie Taylor on second guitar, he appeared in the American singles chart on numerous other occasions. He also made the U.K. singles chart with 'Shame Shame Shame' in September 1964 – it peaked at No. 45. Other than B.B. King, Reed was the biggest selling blues artist in America. A diagnosis of epilepsy in 1957 did not suppress his enthusiasm for performing and he toured constantly. However, his love of the bottle began to increasingly dominate his

SPECIAL
ALL NITE RAVE
MIDNIGHT TO 6 a.m.
CLUB NOREIK
HIGH ROAD, TOTTENHAM, N.15
PRESENTING—
SATURDAY, OCTOBER 31st
U.S.A. R & B STAR
JIMMY REED
ALSO
STEVE MARRIOTT'S MOMENTS
Tickets in advance 10/-. on night 12/6
SATURDAY, NOVEMBER 7th
JOHN LEE HOOKER
Tickets in advance 10/-. on night 12/6
Apply Club Noreik for membership
Coach parties welcomed

"I dig them because they give me a lot of ideas. I listen to them a lot." ~ *Otis Redding talking about Jimmy Reed and Muddy Waters*

Vee-Jay RECORDS

53-120—Vocal
Time 3:00

Conrad Music
B.M.I.

YOU DON'T HAVE TO GO
(J. Reed)
JIMMY REED
and his Trio

VJ-119

"Our own roots in music come from Negro folk sounds fused with English folk. We always try to do something progressive."

~ Mick Jagger, 1966

live appearances in particular, indeed it's thought his epilepsy was alcohol induced. It was on the back of his British hit that he first toured Britain in 1964, giving his many acolytes in the beat and blues bands the chance to see him first hand. According to Bill Wyman it was quite a night. "While we were away recording at 2120 South Michigan Avenue (Chess Studios) in Chicago, Britain was getting into the blues. Just after I got back from the States, Peter Frampton called to say he was playing at Wallington Public Hall. I went to see Peter and the Herd on 24 November 1964, but imagine my surprise when I found out that Jimmy Reed was on the bill. After I played a couple of songs with The Herd, I sat and chatted with Jimmy. His manager kept on saying that the Stones should record 'Big Boss Man!'" Forty years later Bill Wyman and his band, along with Andy Fairweather Low, are still performing 'Bright Lights Big City' in honor of Jimmy Reed.

Reed influenced many artists, while his easy and relaxed style of playing was very accessible to white audiences. In particular the Rolling Stones featured his music from their very earliest days; they covered Reed's 'Honest I Do' on their first album. But that was far from his only contribution to their repertoire. In late 1962, even before they had signed a record deal, they tried

out Jimmy Reed's 'Close Together' for a demo. In February 1963 they also tried out 'Honey What's Wrong' and 'Bright Lights Big City' in the studio. In their early live shows in the blues clubs of West London they would regularly play 'I Ain't Got You' and 'Hush Hush' as well as the three songs they had tried in the studio.

They were far from the only band or artist that liked Reed's relaxed, deceptively simple style. Both The Pretty

"Mathis James Reed sang, played and composed an enormously influential style of blues based on simplicity and a warm, relaxed sort of charm." ~ *Jim ONeal,* Living Blues *magazine*

'Big Boss Man'; The Animals and Them did versions of 'Bright Lights, Big City,' while artists including Etta James, Little Richard, and Hot Tuna covered 'Baby What You Want Me To Do.' Bob Dylan claimed it was Jimmy's harmonica style, as well as the idea for using the harp holder, that influenced his own playing

During the late 1960's more illness, some self-inflicted through his excessive drinking, curtailed his roadwork but he continued to play during the first half of the 1970s, although mainly around Chicago. Mama Reed had also left him after 20 years, as had his manager, both unable to cope any longer with Reed's alcoholism. In 1976 he died when he suffered an attack of epilepsy while asleep. Sadly it was just as he had overcome his drink problems and was once again appearing on the blues circuit. He was only 51 years old but his body had been ravaged by drink; it was sad that music had lost one of its most influential players just as he was getting things back together.

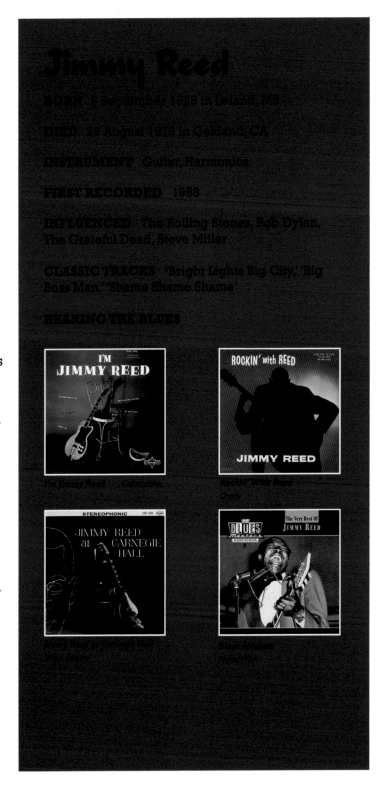

Jimmy Reed

BORN 6 September 1925 in Leland, MS

DIED 29 August 1976 in Oakland, CA

INSTRUMENT Guitar, Harmonica

FIRST RECORDED 1953

INFLUENCED The Rolling Stones, Bob Dylan, The Grateful Dead, Steve Miller

CLASSIC TRACKS 'Bright Lights Big City,' 'Big Boss Man,' 'Shame Shame Shame'

HEARING THE BLUES

I'm Jimmy Reed Collectables

Rockin' With Reed Charly

Jimmy Reed at Carnegie Hall

Blues Masters: The Very Best of

B.B. King

"B.B. King's achievement has been to take the primordial music he heard as a kid, mix and match it with a bewildering variety of other musics, and bring it all into the digital age." ~
Colin Escott, The King of the Blues *box set*

ANY MAN WHO HAS PLAYED over 15,000 gigs in well over 50 years of touring has the right to be called a legend. But B.B. King is a legend for so very much more. He's sold countless records, is respected by musicians everywhere and was named the third-greatest guitarist of all time by *Rolling Stone* magazine, which puts an awful lot of others in the shade. He's also much loved, earning himself the monikers of King of the Blues and Ambassador of the Blues.

Riley B. King is the son of Alfred King and Nora Ella King and he was born in Indianola, deep in the heart of the Mississippi Delta, in 1925. He was named Riley after the Irishman who owned the plantation on which his parents lived and worked. "He was named Jim O'Riley; my dad and Mr O'Riley were such good friends he named me after him, but he left the 'O' off. When I got big enough to know

about it, I asked my dad one day, 'Why is it that you named me after Mr O'Riley, why did you leave the 'O' off?' He said, 'You didn't look Irish enough!'"

According to B.B. King, "Any time you're born on a plantation you have no choice. Plantation first, that's always first." But it was not long before The Beale Street Blues Boy, as Riley B. King became known, sought to change all that. The sharecropper's son first went to Memphis in 1946 and stayed with his cousin Bukka White, but soon returned to Indianola to work as a tractor driver.

Inspired by Sonny Boy Wiliamson's radio show, young Riley moved back to Memphis in 1948. "I got to audition for Sonny Boy, it was one of the Ivory Joe Hunter songs called 'Blues at Sunrise.' Sonny Boy had been working out a little place called the 16th Street Grill down in West Memphis. So he asked the lady that he had been working for, her name was

"My salary, which was the basic salary for us tractor drivers, $22-and-a-half a week, was a lot of money compared to the other people that was working there." ~ *B.B. King*

Miss Annie, 'I'm going to send him down in my place tonight.' My job was to play for the young people that didn't gamble. The 16th Street Grill had a gambling place in the back, if a guy came and brought his girlfriend or his wife that didn't gamble my job was to keep them happy by playing music for them to dance. They seemed to enjoy me playing, so Miss Annie said if you can get a job on the radio like Sonny Boy, I'll give you this job and I'll pay you $12-and-a-half a night. And I'll give you six days of work, room and board. Man I couldn't believe it."

He began working on radio at WDIA in Memphis. "When I was a disc jockey, they use to bill me as 'Blues Boy, the Boy from Beale Street.' People would write me and instead of saying the Blues Boy, they'd just abbreviate it to B.B." His popularity in Memphis earned him the chance to record for Bullet in 1949. His first sides were not too successful, but then Sam Phillips got B.B. into his Memphis Recording Services studio in September 1950. The

Bihari brothers visiting Memphis in search of talent signed B.B. to their RPM label, and agreed to release the sides that he had cut with Phillips. These records failed to catch hold

"We don't play for white people. I'm not saying we won't play for whites, because I don't know what the future holds. Records are funny. You aim them for the colored market, then suddenly the white folks like them, then wham, you've got whites at your dances." ~ *B.B. King during the 1950s*

"I'm trying to get people to see that we are our brother's keeper; red, white, black, brown or yellow, rich or poor, we all have the blues." ~ *B.B. King*

and so Joe Bihari, the youngest brother, went to Memphis and recorded B.B. in a room at the YMCA on 8 January 1951. On a subsequent visit to Memphis, Bihari recorded B.B.'s version of Lowell Fulson's 'Three O'clock Blues.' It entered the chart on 29 December 1951 and eventually spent five weeks at No.1 in early 1952. Not quite an overnight sensation, but it was the start of the most successful long-running career in modern blues history.

In the early years of his success he stayed in Memphis where he was a big star, but not always as big as he thought he was. "We were in Memphis at the Auditorium, Elvis was there watching and performing were Bobby Bland, Little Milton, Little Junior Parker, Howlin' Wolf and myself. Everybody had been on stage. Bobby Bland, a stage mover man, he can move the people, Little Milton and myself, you know we do what we do but we couldn't move the crowd quickly like Bobby Bland. We had been on and now Howlin' Wolf is up and the people are going crazy.

Milton says, 'Something is going on out there.' Junior Parker says 'Let's check it out.' So Wolf is doing 'Spoonful,' now we go out there and he's on his knees crawling round on the floor. The people just going crazy so finally we figured out what it was; the seat of his pants was busted! And all of his business is hanging out!"

One night while B.B. was playing at a club in Twist, Arkansas there was a fight and a stove was knocked over which set fire to the wooden building. The band and audience had rushed outside before King realized that he had left his beloved $30 guitar inside; rushing back into the burning building he managed to get his guitar even though he almost died in the process. It turned out the fight was over a woman named Lucille – which is how B.B.'s guitar got its name; every one of his 20 or so custom-made Gibson guitars has been called Lucille.

Throughout the time King recorded for RPM he churned out hit after hit, topping the R&B chart

"Well B.B. was like a hero. The band? You listen to the way that band swings on *Live at The Regal*, it's just like a steamroller."

~ *Mick Fleetwood*

three more times, until he left RPM for Kent in late 1958. King's sojourn at Kent lasted throughout much of the 60s, and while he never again topped the R&B charts he had many hits. His sweet, gospel-tinged voice coupled with his brilliant single-string picking proved an irresistible combination. It made King one of THE most successful artists on the R&B charts for all time.

By the late 1960s B.B., like his fellow blues-guitar players, was discovered by the young white rock fraternity, which gave his career a a real boost. In 1970 'The Thrill is Gone' made No. 3 on the R&B chart. It also crossed over to the Hot 100 and became his biggest hit when it made No. 15. In 1969 he visited Europe for the first of many tours; audiences, well aware of the legend's influence on Eric Clapton, Peter Green et al, readily accepted him. King's album *Live at the Regal*, recorded in 1964, had long been held in high esteem by both musicians and fans alike, on both sides of the Atlantic.

Much of B.B.'s success can be attributed to his live shows. He has always been one of the hardest-working live performers, playing 250–300 dates a year, even in some of the lean years. He also has a knack for keeping his bands together, an indication of his skill as a bandleader, but probably a lot to do with his gracious nature as a boss. As B.B. himself said in 2000, "The guys are not only great musicians, they're loyal to me, I'm loyal to them, and we get together and have a good time. Everybody's

been with me a long time, my late drummer, Sonny Freeman was with me around 18 years and now my senior trumpeter has been with me 21 years and everybody, except one, has been with me more than 10 years."

In 1969 B.B toured America with the Rolling Stones, which for many would have been the first time they had seen one of the all-time greats in the flesh. According to Bill Wyman, "We used to go on side stage and watch B.B. play. He had a 12-piece band and they were brilliant musicians. The thing that always stunned me about his playing was the way he hammered it out and then he'd just go down to a whisper. There was just silence in the place, you could hear a pin drop. He would suddenly start to build it to a big climax, that's what I liked about his playing, the dimensions of his music."

Throughout the 1970s, when many others found it difficult to find decent work, King was always there or thereabouts. He even appeared on TV, when almost no other blues artists could get a look in. His reputation with other guitarists gave him the position of elder statesman of the blues. Added to which he has always been articulate in explaining the meaning of the blues, and in so doing he helped keep the fire burning when it had all but gone out. There has been criticism of King as being too smooth for the blues; sour grapes from those would have given anything to achieve a modicum of his success.

In 1988, the year after he was inducted into the

Rock and Roll Hall of Fame, King worked with U2 on their album *Rattle & Hum*. His performance on 'When Love Comes to Town' proved he still had it, even at 63 years old. This was not the first time King played with others. In the 1970s he played with jazz group The Crusaders, and others he has worked with have included the blind singer Diane Schuur, Alexis Korner, Stevie Winwood and Bobby Bland. In 2001 B.B. King and his long-time friend Eric Clapton won a Grammy award for their album, *Riding With The King*. Among the covers on the album are

'Worried Life Blues' and 'Key To The Highway' while they also revisited 'Three O'Clock Blues.'

B.B. King, like many of his contemporaries, was inspired by Louis Jordan to believe that a black musician could achieve great things, and for many years B.B. spoke of wanting to record an album of the legendary bandleader's material.

In 1999 he released that album, which both acknowledges his debt to Louis and celebrates the King of the Jukebox's string of great hit records. The album's title, appropriately, is *Let the Good Times Roll*. It's also the song that B.B. King has used to open his live shows for decades.

King's great skill has been to ride out the mood swings of modern music and continue to come up with interesting albums. He brought the blues out of the margins and into the mainstream of American music. He, above all others, is the undisputed King of the Blues.

B.B. King

BORN 16 September 1925 in Indianola, MS

INSTRUMENT Guitar

FIRST RECORDED 1949

INFLUENCES Robert Johnson, Blind Lemon Jefferson, T-Bone Walker, Stephanne Grapelli, Sonny Boy Williamson

INFLUENCED Eric Clapton, Otis Rush, Albert Collins, Johnny Winter

CLASSIC TRACKS 'Three O'Clock Blues,' 'Sweet Angel,' 'The Thrill Is Gone'

HEARING THE BLUES

Live At The Regal   MCA

Do The Boogie, Early 50s
Classics   Virgin

Riding With The King
Reprise/WEA

The RPM Hits 1951-1957
Ace Records

Second
B
B
KING'S
BLUES
CLUB
Memphis
Records, Tapes & Souvenirs
SAM'S TOWN
800-456-0711
ASK FOR
SPEED LIMIT 25
ONE WAY
NO PARKING STANDING ANYTIME
ATM
Third

The Music on the CD

1. **The Gallis Pole**
(Ledbetter/Lomax) Kensington Music Ltd.
Lead Belly's song was recorded in New York City on 1 April 1939. Led Zeppelin covered it in 1970 on their third album; it does not credit Lead Belly or Alan Lomax as the writers; it just says it's a traditional song arranged by Plant and Page.

2. **Shake it and Break It (But Don't Let it Fall Mama)** *(Patton) Public Domain work*
Recorded by Charley Patton on 14 June 1929 on his first trip to the Richmond, Indiana studio of Paramount Records.

3. **Blind Arthur's Breakdown**
(Blake) Copyright Control
Blind Blake first recorded in 1926 for the Paramount label. Three years later in October 1929 he recorded this wonderful instrumental track and was credited on the label as Blind Arthur.

4. **Key To The Highway**
(Broonzy/Segar) Universal/MCA Music Ltd.
Recorded by Big Bill Broonzy for the Okeh label on Friday 2 May 1941, it also features Washboard Sam on his preferred instrument and Jazz Gillum on harmonica. Eric Clapton later covered it on his *Layla and Other Assorted Love Songs* album.

5. **'Tain't Nobody's Business If I Do**
(Grainger & Robbins) EMI Music Publishing Ltd.
Bessie Smith recorded this blues classic accompanied by Clarence Williams on piano in late April 1923.

6. **Matchbox Blues**
(Jefferson) Public Domain work
Blind Lemon Jefferson recorded this in April 1927 for the Paramount label. Thirty-seven years later, on a Monday in June 1964, Ringo Starr, along with the rest of The Beatles, recorded a song called 'Matchbox' in London's Abbey Road Studios. The Beatles learned the song from the version that Carl Perkins had recorded in 1956; he based his song on Blind Lemon's 29-year-old bestseller.

7. **Me and My Chauffeur Blues**
(Lawler) Universal/MCA Music Ltd.
Memphis Minnie recorded this classic along with Little Son Joe and an unknown bass player on Wednesday 21 May 1941 in Chicago for the Okeh label. It would prove to be an enduring inspiration for many who came later.

8. **Don't Start Me Talkin'**
(Williamson) Tristan Music Ltd.
Sonny Boy Williamson's only significant hit was this song that made No.3 on the *Billboard* chart in 1955.

9. **Statesboro Blues**
(McTell) Peermusic UK Ltd.
Blind Willie McTell recorded this much-covered blues song at his second session for the Victor label in Atlanta Georgia on 17 October 1928. He cut four songs in total that day, just like he did at his first session a year earlier.

10. **Walking Blues**

(House) Bug Music Ltd.

Son House recorded this song at his first session for Paramount on Wednesday 28 May 1930 in Grafton, Wisconsin; Willie Brown accompanied him on guitar.

11. **Let Me Play With Your Poodle**

(Whittaker) Universal/MCA Music Ltd.

Recorded by Tampa Red for the Bluebird label on Friday 6 February 1942, this also features Clifford 'Snags' Jones on drums.

12. **Call It Stormy Monday (But Tuesday Is Just As Bad)**

(Walker) Burlington Music Ltd.

Recorded in Hollywood in mid-1947 for the Black and White label, this classic slice of T-Bone Walker also features Oscar Lee Bradley on drums, Arthur Edwards on bass, pianist Lloyd Glen, tenor sax player Bump Meyers and Teddy Buckner on trumpet.

13. **Smokestack Lightnin'**

(Chester Burnett) Jewel Music Publishing Company Ltd.

Howlin' Wolf recorded this at Chess Records in Chicago in January 1956, accompanied by Willie Dixon on bass, Hubert Sumlin on guitar, Hosea Lee Kennard on piano, Earl Phillips on drums and guitarist Willie Johnson.

14. **Me and The Devil Blues**

(Johnson) Kobalt Music Publishing Ltd.

This Robert Johnson song comes from his last session, recorded in Dallas on Sunday 20 June 1937.

15. **Coffee Blues**

(Ellen) Molique Music

This Lightnin' Hopkins song was recorded in New York City sometime in 1951.

16. **I'm Your Hoochie Coochie Man**

(Dixon) Jewel Music Publishing Company Ltd & Bug Music Ltd.

Muddy Waters accompanied by Walter Horton on harmonica, Jimmy Rogers on guitar, drummer Elgar Edwards, and bassist Big Crawford and recorded in Chicago in 1953.

17. **Boogie Chillen'**

(Hooker/Besman) Universal Music Publishing & Sony/ATV Publishing (UK).

John Lee Hooker recorded this on a September day in 1948 in a studio in Detroit; it's a record that changed the face of modern music. Bernard Besman, the owner of the Sensation label, leased Hooker's first two sides to Modern Records; it went to No. 1 on the R&B chart in January 1949.

18. **Dust My Broom**

(Johnson arr. James) Tristan Music Ltd & Kobalt Music Publishing Ltd.

Elmore James, along with Sonny Boy Williamson on harmonica, Odie Johnson on bass and Frock O'Dell on drums, cut this in Jackson, Mississippi in 1952 for the Trumpet label.

19. **Honest I Do**

(Reed/Abner) Tristan Music Ltd.

Jimmy Reed was in a Chicago studio on 3 April 1957 along with Eddie Taylor on guitar and Earl Phillips on drums, to cut this classic side for the Vee-Jay label.

20. **Three O'Clock Blues**

(Fulson) Sony/ATV Publishing (UK).

Recorded in Memphis in 1951 for the RPM label, this became B.B. King's first big hit recording when it went to No. 1 on the *Billboard* Rhythm & Blues chart in early 1952, staying there for five weeks.

Further Reading & Web Sites

Some of these books are out of print, but well worth searching out. If you're looking for out-of-print books why not try www.addall.com

Crying for the Carolines by Bruce Bastin (Blues Paperbacks)
Shining Trumpets by Rudi Blesh (Cassell)
King of the Delta Blues – The Life & Music of Charley Patton by Stephen Calt & Gayle Wardlow (Rock Chapel Press)
The Country Blues by Samuel B. Charters (Da Capo)
The Poetry of the Blues by Samuel B. Charters (Oak Publications)
Woman with a Guitar – Memphis Minnie's Blues by Paul & Beth Garon (Da Capo)
Searching for Robert Johnson by Peter Guralnick (Plume Books)
Feel Like Going Home by Peter Guralnick (Penguin)
In Search of the Blues by Marybeth Hamilton
Blues People by Le Roi Jones (The Jazz Book Club)
The Land Where the Blues Began by Alan Lomax (Minerva)
Yonder Comes The Blues by Paul Oliver, Tony Russell, Robert M.W. Dixon, John Godrich & Howard Rye (Cambridge University Press)
Blues Fell This Morning by Paul Oliver (Cambridge University Press)
Conversation with the Blues by Paul Oliver (Cambridge University Press)
The Story of the Blues by Paul Oliver (Pimlico)
Deep Blues by Robert Palmer (Penguin)
Chicago Blues by Mike Rowe (Da Capo)
The Arrival of B.B. King by Charles Sawyer (Doubleday)
Chasin' The Devil's Music by Gayle Wardlow (Backbeat Books)
Bill Wyman's Blues Odyssey by Bill Wyman & Richard Havers (Dorling Kindersley)

WEB SITES
The Blues Foundation: www.blues.org
The Blue Highway: www.thebluehighway.com
The Blues Trail: www.thebluestrail.com
Document Records: www.document-records.com
You'll find probably the most comprehensive list of blues links available anywhere at Blues World. Check it out: www.bluesworld.com

The statue of Elvis Aaron Presley, 'The King of Rock'n'Roll,' on Beale Street at Main, Memphis, TN

> **"Well, the blues had a baby, and they named the baby rock'n'roll."**
> ~ *Muddy Waters*

Index